REWIRE YOUR
BUSINESS
FOR SUCCESS

The 6-step method to increase
profit and reclaim your freedom

ELENA MESKHI

RETHINKPRESS

First published in Great Britain in 2020 by
Rethink Press (www.rethinkpress.com)

Praise

Elena has hit the target with this easy-to-read guide to the highs and lows of the early years of ownership and how to run a clever business.

Whether you are thinking of setting up from scratch, have been in business for a few short years, or you are experienced but hitting a glass ceiling, *Rewire Your Business For Success* will be a breath of fresh air – an experienced accountant sharing her observations and top tips based on years in the trenches with her clients.

Elena isn't just an accountant, she is a pragmatic business coach who has seen at first hand the challenges of small businesses (having built her own) and is full of smart ideas to maximise productivity, profitability and personal effectiveness.

Reading *Rewire Your Business For Success* and learning Elena's six principles will turbo-charge the enthusiasm you have for your own business, by sharing techniques that will allow you to put yourself first, whilst continuing to deliver first-class service.

This book will be added to my recommended reading list for clients.
> — **Chris Barrow,** Business Coach, Speaker and Writer

Elena has written an invaluable business resource for established SMEs with revenues between £150k and £2.5M and employing 3-25 staff. Her proven six-step strategic method for growing the value of a business, retaining more net profits and improving net cashflow combines well with informed guidance on finding, selecting and working with a proactive accountant. This does not replace competent accountancy but will improve the quality of the service agreement and what you should expect from your accountant. Importantly, this book provides the strategy and steps to set up a business that delivers more cash... and life... sooner and bigger.
> — **Andrew Priestley,** The Coaching Experience/Dent Global

The theme of small business development and coaching for small and medium entrepreneurs is a very hot topic in today's literature. However, Elena's book stands out distinctly from the crowd. Her formidable strategy of sharing with the reader a first-hand experience of what not to do and why not to do so is indeed a cornerstone of the book. The references to her own mistakes, setbacks and real-life examples send a powerful message to an audience that, after reading the book, will definitely be reflecting on their own actions through ideas from the book.

— **Dr. Evgeny Kunts,** CFSA, MCSI, London City

To my husband, Tim. This book was inspired, created, written and produced – as are many things in my life – thanks to you.

Contents

Introduction

I moved to the UK from Russia because I liked the sense of freedom, attitude and culture. My economics degree alone was not enough to practise accountancy here, so I needed to get an accredited professional qualification too. I had enough determination to get my practising certificate but, to get on the career ladder, I also needed experience. Unfortunately, because I didn't have any experience in the UK, I couldn't get a job. Of course, without a job, it's impossible to gain experience. It's a vicious cycle that a lot of young graduates in this profession will encounter. In addition, at that time there was prejudice against some nationalities, Russians included, when it came to offering jobs. I couldn't find a way out of this situation until one innovative accountancy practice launched a programme that gave accountancy students the opportunity to work with them to gain experience. There was a catch: I had to pay half of my monthly salary for the opportunity. I decided to take it anyway, doing everything from secretarial and receptionist duties to analytical reviews and learning about software.

I gained my experience in that firm while I was studying and working part time at other places. I was accumulating the knowledge and skills I wanted, and it felt absolutely fantastic: my life was full-on and I loved it. The firm was comparatively large, with nine partners and about eighty employees. Because the firm was so innovative, they were exploring opportunities in the Russian market and were hoping to secure a big contract to do a few years of auditing for a group of companies.

They asked if I would like to join them on the trip to Russia because my language skills would be useful. Accepting the offer was a no-brainer for me! We met the board of directors of the Russian company and, although they were interested in what was being proposed to them, it was clear to me, being Russian, that they were starting to get bored and that the UK firm was in danger of losing them. I could see that they were moving the conversation in completely the wrong way. During a break in the meeting, I asked my boss if he would trust me to continue the negotiations. He agreed, and as a result we won the contract: two to three years of solid work. My boss was delighted, and on the way back to London he offered me the position of trainee accountant and auditor. I worked with that company for five years, qualified with them and was eventually promoted to a management position.

To broaden my experience, I decided to go into industry, and I joined an oil trading company as a financial controller. Within months it became clear to me that there was a lot of duplication across the company so, with the management's permission, I began to simplify their processes. Using technology, I saved the company £500,000 a year by making five people redundant and offering to work part time on a contracting basis to implement their new systems. That's how I came to set up my own company, and this firm was my first client.

I am now a certified accountant and tax advisor in the UK and lead a team of accountants and tax professionals in London. Besides this, I own and run a few other businesses in different industries. I also sit on the boards of bigger companies, providing them with insights and expertise in finance and accounting.

I love learning about different industries and how they operate. Even though I'm a certified accountant, I look at a business from the owner's perspective. I have opened, sold and closed a number of businesses, earning money from some and making a loss on others. I have learned so much from each deal, and some of the less profitable ones have taught me far more valuable lessons than any profit-making deal has. That is why I have so much to share.

Who is this book for?

I have done a lot of business development training in my career. Every time I invested my time and attention in training, I faced the same problem: I felt guilty for not working *in* my business. To be able to take my business to the next level, taking the time to go through that training was not only beneficial, but essential. I understood that the sacrifice was necessary, but at the same time my team needed me and the operational side of my business would suffer to some extent, leading to more feelings of guilt. Eventually, I had an epiphany: for a business owner to be able to take business development courses or be away from the office for other reasons, they need to bulletproof their business and their mind. This book is written precisely to help you do that.

This book is for businesses that are operating in the service industries, have been in business for three to five years and have a turnover of between £150,000 and £2,500,000. This includes medical services, dental services, chiropractors, IT consultancy services, marketing agencies, architects, interior designers, land-scape designers and many more. This book is for business owners who, regardless of turn-over, are still working long hours and doing all the tasks in the business. It will help you to free up your time so you can work 'on' the business rather than 'in' it and spend more time with your family or doing the things you love.

This book is for people who are moving their business from the start-up stage to the ado-lescence stage. There are already many books available to guide you through the start-up stage, and if you are considering setting up a new business you should read some of them for help and advice. One book I recommend is *Wealth Without the Job* by Andy Fuehl.

The problem

I have found that when people set up a busi-ness they have two drivers in mind: cash and freedom. The first driver is to get more cash. Many people think that once they have started a business, they will be in control of the cash; if they want more cash then all they need to do is work a few more hours. Once they are OK for cash, they can step back and work a bit less, gaining freedom. They believe that being their own boss will allow them to spend more time with family or working on their personal goals. In reality, they end up working 24/7 and chasing a horizon that moves faster than they do. They look after their clients, their employees and their suppliers, without prioritising their own needs. I know this because I have done the same: I have become frantic about looking after everybody but myself. As business owners, we neglect our personal needs because we are so preoccupied with business.

In this book I will share my knowledge by showing you my step-by-step model to rewire your business for success. As you're doing this, you will also rewire your brain – if the neurons are firing together, they're wiring together.

It's about building new habits and getting rid of old. Any habit we have or any action we do creates the neuron connection in our brain.

This is how the brain works. The more often we do the action the stronger the neuron connection. At some point you begin running on 'autopilot' – that's why it's so difficult to break old habits. Do you remember step-by-step how you got to the office today? Probably not, because you have done it so many times before and at some point, your autopilot has switched on. In this book I will help you to identify your old business autopilot scenarios which no longer serve your business well. Instead we will establish a new routine and new habits which will take over and grow your business.

What you will get from this book

This book sets out six principles to help you overcome problems by rewiring your business for success. Here is an overview of what you will find in each chapter:

Chapter 1 – Learn about the three key problems that every business owner encounters and how a good accountant can help you turn your business around.

Chapter 2 – Principle 1: Pay Yourself First. When you apply this principle, you will transform your mindset and your business.

Chapter 3 – Principle 2: Stocktake. Learn how to evaluate your business and plan your strategy to deal with the problems you are facing.

Chapter 4 – Principle 3: Rewire. Find out how to create new routines that will lead to improvements in your business and stop you repeating the patterns that have kept you stuck in a rut.

Chapter 5 – Principle 4: Automate. Discover key ways to automate your processes and find out how your accountant can help you implement your strategy smoothly.

Chapter 6 – Principle 5: Optimise. Learn how to get the most value from your accountant. Isn't that what every business owner wants to know?

Chapter 7 – Principle 6: Protect. This is the most important step for any business owner. I will show you the key ways to protect yourself and your business, now and in the future.

How to use this book

This is a practical book that will have an impact on your business as you work through it. It is vital that you read through each chapter in order because the book builds on previous advice, so you miss out on concepts by dipping into the chapters indiscriminately. More importantly, you must act. You will find exercises throughout this book, which I urge you to stop and complete.

This book will guide you through a process. You might be tempted to jump to the middle if one subject is of more interest to you than another. Please resist this temptation: the process is designed so that each step builds on the previous one. Going through the stages in sequence will help you to review your business on different levels.

You might find one step easier than another, but that doesn't make it any more or less important: it just means that part of your business is in better shape. By making a few extra tweaks, you will improve it even further – and those tweaks might be the catalyst that rockets your business into the stratosphere. On the other hand, you might find some sections difficult and resist doing them. We are creatures of habit, so when we try to do things differently our body and mind rebel. If you have difficulty with certain stages, reach out to me so that I can guide you through. Please find my contact details at the end of this book.

ONE

Problems for the
Business Owner

Three main problems prevent business owners from having successful profitable businesses. When they collide, these problems create disorganisation and chaos, resulting in tasks not getting done or being done erratically. The business owner's aspiration for a better work-life balance fades as they find themselves working harder and for longer hours just to keep the business afloat. In this chapter, I will identify those problems and look at how working with a good accountant can get your company back on the path to achieving your business and personal goals.

Three key problems

In my years of experience as an accountant, I have worked with the full spectrum of businesses – from start-ups to well-developed companies that have been established for more than five years. I have assisted clients in starting from scratch and developing strategies to grow organically or acquire other businesses, and I have valued businesses for the purpose of selling, buying, raising funding and even listing at the London Stock Exchange. Time and again, three problems crop up in my conversations with clients, and it is these that are preventing them from achieving success.

Those problems are **cash, systems and team.**

Let's look at each of these in more detail.

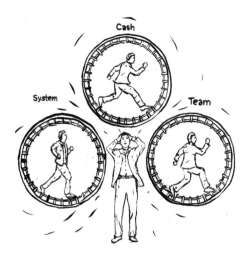

Business owner in distress

Cash

When I say 'cash', I mean the lack of it. If a business has enough cash, then this is not a problem. If a business doesn't have enough cash, it is because their systems either do not work or are inconsistent. Without effective systems in place, your cash-flow problems will only become obvious when your expenses exceed your income – something that happens when you pay the bills too soon. Some business owners, believing that they're taking a common-sense approach, pay all their bills as quickly as possible. Their aim is to keep everyone happy, but in doing so they are making things more stressful for themselves. We'll look at a better approach to paying invoices in Chapter Two.

Cash is the lifeblood of any business, so it's vital to understand how it operates and what to do with it when you earn it. First, and most importantly, you need to pay yourself. Then you can put reserves aside so you can invest to grow your business. Many business owners think that they should wait until they have built up a reserve before they even start to think about investing or paying themselves. As a consequence, they never have enough money in the bank and never succeed in creating a profitable business.

It's important to take that leap of faith and create a cash-handling process that allows you to pay yourself first and put funds aside to develop your business and invest, all at the same time. There's no need to wait for that magical moment when your business has earned enough and you can make a fat payment to yourself. You need to create that moment now, and I will show you how.

Systems

These are your systems for sending invoices, paying expenses, sending quotes, handling complaints and so on. These processes have to be systematised so that they can be done consistently regardless of who is following them. I've never met a business owner who doesn't have a problem with their systems. That's because systems can be complex, but when you put them in place properly they make a huge difference to how you operate, which makes your life much easier. As with any big improvement, it's the complexity of setting them up that causes the headache. My motto is that simplifying as much as possible will give you the best results.

Unfortunately, problems with systems are compounded by the business owner who does not delegate. They have their own way of doing things; they might believe that they are the best person to handle the client relationship or to deliver their service. In reality, though, one person cannot do everything. It is only when they have a team member who they can trust that the business owner starts to feel that they can hand these systems over. The new employee becomes a 'mini-me' and imitates all aspects of what the business owner does.

The danger here is that employees will create their own systems. This happens if an employee hasn't been given all the steps in a process. If a process has been developed through trial and error and the business owner has never recorded in writing how they do things, a team member who takes over a particular process will apply their own knowledge and expertise. As a result, the system may be altered and it will be difficult for anyone else to replicate it in their absence, causing chaos and stress for the business owner and the rest of the team.

The only way to create perfect systems is to write down everything you do and review it with your team every quarter or at least every six months. Principle 4, Automate, gives you advice on the systems your business needs for seamless financial operations. You will be amazed by the impact that good systems can have on your business.

Team

This is your extended team, which includes not only full-time employees but also freelancers and partners that support the business: your solicitor, accountant, tax advisor or marketing consultant. Business owners should also consider themselves as part of the team.

Sadly, the business owner can also be part of the problem. They have strong ideas about what is best – after all, it is their business. They are the experts in their fields, and they know their niche and industry inside out. They are perfectionists: believing that their approach is right, they refuse to delegate and end up doing everything themselves. They become disorganised because they are too busy, creating chaos around them by slowing things down and often paralysing the business.

The problems relating to cash, systems and team overlap and can result in burnout for the business owner. They don't enjoy their work anymore, and they feel depressed and anxious. They are too exhausted to go to work. Everything irritates them about their business, even though they are proud of it and passionate about it. The secret is that these three circles are meant to work like a well-oiled machine. When they don't, they get stuck and the business owner ends up chasing their tail without achieving anything.

Beliefs about accountants

I've become aware of several myths that have developed among business owners about what an accountant does and does not do. It's important to dispel these myths here and now, because they may be holding you back from working with good accountants who can help your business flourish.

Myth 1: Accountants have successful businesses

An accountant is just like any other business owner. They may or may not be running a successful business. They experience the same problems as other business owners, and they often operate in the same disorganised way. It is likely that someone in your business network has recommended an accountant to you. You will never know if that accountant is in the same chaotic state as you are or if they too are experiencing cash-flow problems: an accountant will never acknowledge that their own business is in disarray. This type of accountant is in no position to help you sort out your own problems, because they don't see disorganised ways of working or cash-flow problems as an issue. They will say that having problems with cash flow is part of owning a business, because they are in the same position as you are.

This is not how it should be. If you have a strategy for your business and you have good partners, including a good accountant, you won't have a problem with cash flow. As they say, if you're the smartest person in the room then you're in the wrong room. You want to surround yourself with people you can learn from, so choose an accountant who has the mindset of a successful business owner and runs a successful business.

Myth 2: Accountants are only good with figures

I have lost count of the number of times people have said that because I'm an accountant, I must be good with figures. Yes, I am good with numbers, but I am also good with people and building relationships. I'm good with aspects of law, marketing and many other business-related skills. The image of the accountant as someone who sits in an office crunching numbers all day implies that they can't help or advise you on anything else. This is untrue. Because of the breadth of experience that a good accountant will have, they will be able to advise you on most business issues, such as growing your team, creating a plan for the future, developing your business strategy and increasing your profits. A good accountant makes a great business coach.

Myth 3: I only need an accountant to prepare my tax return

This is true if your accountant says they'll see you in nine months' time with your box of receipts. That said, why would you need nine months to prepare your accounts if your accountant had supported you to set up your business in an organised and systematic way? In part, this myth has developed because most accountants in the UK are not hands-on in their client's business. In other countries the accountant looks after the business accounts and financial affairs. In such countries it's the director's duty to engage an accountant (employed or outsourced) because it's implied by the positions: the director should run the company and the accountant should maintain the books of the company. In Russia, for example, the accountant and the director are of equal importance in the company.

In reality, your accountant can do far more for your business than simply preparing your tax return. Accountants are the best-placed people to advise you on setting up systems to ensure your cash flows so you have enough to run and grow your business. To do this properly, they need to be part of your team right from day one. Choose someone who is supportive and who can take the time to explain, give guidance and highlight how you can deliver your services so that your business will prosper.

Myth 4: Business owners can do their own accounting

Software companies have unintentionally widened the gap between the business owner and the accountant by developing bookkeeping products such as Xero, QuickBooks, Sage and FreeAgent. These companies have invested millions of pounds in making their products attractive, useful and so user-friendly that children can use them. They've also invested in marketing to show business owners that doing the bookkeeping is easy and straightforward. That's absolutely true: thanks to the dramatic improvements in the technology available, recording and sorting invoices is no longer a task to be dreaded.

Somehow, though, the message that it's a great idea to automate invoicing and expense-handling in real-time has led business owners to believe that they can do their own accounting. I receive a large number of enquiries from enthusiasts who are doing their own bookkeeping, accounting and sometimes even tax planning. Unfortunately, the quality of the work shows that this is a myth. In many cases, when preparing annual company accounts from data that was prepared by clients who do their own bookkeeping, I have had to redo twelve months' worth of VAT returns that had been done incorrectly.

Technology can make some bookkeeping tasks easier for business owners, but it is no substitute for a qualified accountant. Accountants must study for at least five years to qualify. In my case, on coming to the UK I took a professional qualification to become accredited as an accountant here, which took another three years. I also worked as a trainee accountant to learn new skills and gain experience for my studies. Accountants can apply and analyse your financial information far more effectively than software can, and they can use that information to help you grow your business. As you are an expert in your field, so too are they.

I'm not suggesting that you need to have an accountant in-house: that would be costly. Instead, you can outsource to someone who you can consult and who can guide you through business financial processes. Having an experienced accountant on board can dramatically expand your business.

Myth 5: I only need an accountant to look after my business

That can't be further from the truth. The business owner and the business are a unit, and your accountant will only be doing half the job if they deal with your business in isolation. How your business operates depends on you, and you depend on your business. Here are two examples that show how your accountant can make a difference to both your business and you.

EXAMPLE: PERSONAL ALLOWANCE

The standard payment structure for the company director is to pay them the minimum wage so that they can use up their personal allowance during the year. At the end of the financial year, the business owner, as a shareholder, receives dividends from the business.

This sounds simple, but if the business owner has any other sources of income (for example, from rent) then the strategy for getting a salary from the business will no longer include the personal allowance. That fact alone shows that the business owner's personal finances will affect their strategy.

EXAMPLE: REMORTGAGING

Consider a business owner who gets a salary and dividends from the business and wants to remortgage their home. The business owner would have to apply to the bank, but the fact that they receive a salary and dividends might not appeal to their bank.

An accountant would be able to advise the business owner on the changes they would need to make for the bank to accept their remortgage application.

The accountant's duties

Share expertise on running the business

Having dispelled a few myths about accountants, let's look at exactly what an accountant's duty is to you as a client. Firstly, they shouldn't open a company for you and then tell you to come back in twelve months with your record books or a box of receipts. Their duty is to help you find solutions to any problems you are having in your business or to set up the business and advise on strategies for running it. There are different solutions for different scenarios within and between businesses. If you own a product-based business, you might need a different bank account from a company that deals in international trade, for example. An accountant who has experience of working with a broad range of businesses will be able to see where one solution might work and another won't, and they can use that expertise to help you develop business strategies that meet your specific needs.'

If you are an accountant, you might tell me that you are not licensed to give advice on banking or financial products – and you would be right. I am not suggesting that you step outside what you are allowed to do, but that you share the information that you have learned from your clients with other business owners. If you know of one bank that doesn't charge an arm and a leg for foreign transactions, it is common sense that you share that information. You are not promoting that bank or selling their products; you are simply using your knowledge of what is happening in the market to help your clients decide how best to build a successful business.

As an expert in their field, a business owner focuses on the work they do. They don't have time to research different bank accounts. A dentist, for example, thinks mainly about their patients – their root canals, fillings and treatment plans. There is little room left for thinking about invoicing and card payments. A good accountant, who is fulfilling their duty, will give that dentist advice on payment systems, banking, good platforms to use and which of those platforms are cheaper. It is the accountant's job to share knowledge so that their clients can make the best choices for them. The conversation shouldn't be limited to tax returns.

Broaden your view of the industry

Of course, your accountant has a duty to prepare your accounts, but I would argue that they should then compare them with the industry to benchmark your business with others in the sector and give you an idea of the position and status of your company. Your accountant should let you know how you are doing, tell you what profit you should be looking at and guide you on how much of a margin you need to put on a service for the business to be viable. That's because you can only judge your success by the amount of money you have in your pocket.

Help you achieve financial freedom

One of the most common questions new clients ask me is 'How can I pay less tax?' When I dive deeper into this, I find that it isn't about greed or wanting to avoid paying tax; it's another way of saying 'How can I generate or keep more profit?' This is another way of addressing their cash-flow problem. Usually, a client who wants to pay less tax is not earning enough profit. They are not against paying tax, but they don't have enough money to meet their business and, in turn, their personal needs. In my opinion, it is your accountant's duty to raise those subjects and talk to you about how you can achieve financial freedom.

Create a winning strategy

When I start working with new clients, they often tell me that the solution to their problems and the breakthrough for their business is to attract more leads and convert them into clients. Sometimes, this is the only strategy for the business. The irony is that this can't be further from the truth for a business that has been operating for at least three years.

When I ask the business owner how many more clients they will need to solve their problems, they might answer something like this:

> 'We need ten more clients who pay us £5,000 for a project, but then I'll need one more assistant to help me to work on those extra projects and the assistant will have a salary of at least £25,000. And we'll need a computer (another £1,000) and we're going to have a recruitment cost (another £3,000). Then we're going to have £21,000 left from that stream…'

At this point, the business owner realises that having ten more clients will mean an extra five hours' work a day – and when that business owner already works nine hours a day, the prospect of ten new clients is no longer as appealing. By concentrating on attracting new clients, the business owner moves even further away from their original driver when starting the business: freedom.

Your accountant is the best person to discuss your business strategy with. Every business owner needs to have a strategy that covers how services are priced, how to deal with income and expenses, how to accumulate reserves for the business and where and when to invest. Your accountant knows what the sales price is made up of, what salaries the business is paying, what the overheads are and what the profit should be. Once they have helped you to create a strategy, you will be able to see the full picture of how your business works. In short, this is where a good accountant makes the difference.

Most business owners will say their 'big why' for starting a business was to work less and earn more. This is exactly what a successful business achieves. Successful entrepreneurs have found a balance between how much time they spend on their business and how much time they spend doing other things that they want to do. To achieve this, you need to have good financial planning in place. The method and tools explained in this book will help you do just that by reviewing your business as it stands and developing a strategy for getting you to where you want to be.

As you continue reading, you will learn more about this method. For now, here is an overview of the six principles.

The first principle – **Pay Yourself First** – is the first and most crucial step to transforming your life and your business.

The second principle is **Stocktake**. At this stage, you establish the exact position of your business and set goals for where you want it to be. You'll look at three aspects of your life – financial, business and personal – and come up with some exciting discoveries.

The third principle is **Rewire**. Once you have a picture of your business in the past, present and future, it's time to create a strategy for achieving what you want. This means looking in detail at every process in your business and making them more refined.

The fourth principle is **Automate**. This is about finding the easiest and quickest way to implement your strategy so you can achieve faster results. To do this, you might need to make some small changes in your business, but never underestimate the power of those tweaks: they could be what makes it possible for your business to take off.

Once this is finished, you'll be able to see that you're moving towards the business of your dreams. With your new systems in place, all the wheels will be spinning in the right direction and you'll no longer feel trapped. This is when your accountant can make a real impact on your business.

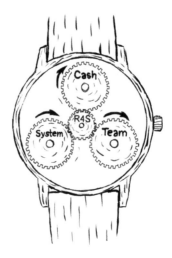

The fifth principle is **Optimise**. This is about learning how to optimise your tax liabilities, how to plan your business so that your company pays your expenses, and how you can keep most of the profit that your business earns. Now you will have total clarity around what you are earning, how much you are spending and how much you are retaining. Working through this Optimise stage will change your business so that eventually you'll have enough money to maintain the lifestyle you want.

Once you've built a successful business, what's important is to protect your assets. This leads to the sixth principle: **Protect**. This is about how you can protect yourself and your business, whether it is making a profit or a loss, and how you can expand it safely. It's about learning who you need to protect your business from and what you can do to prevent stressful situations from arising.

In the chapters that follow, we will dive deep into each principle. I will explain why you need to go through each stage and how to do so simply and effectively. Join me on this journey to find out more about what takes place at each stage.

Summary

In this chapter we have covered the three key problems encountered by business owners:

- Cash

- Systems

- Teams

We've dispelled the myths about accountants and looked at the accountant's duty to you as a client. You have been introduced to the six principles to rewire your business for success.

Before you continue the next chapter, complete the following exercise.

EXERCISE: SCORE HOW YOUR BUSINESS IS DOING AT THE MOMENT

Fill in your scorecard at www.rewire4success. com/book/scorecard. This online tool will give you an objective score for how your business is doing at this moment in time.

When you've completed the scorecard, you'll receive a report on the next steps you should take to rewire your business for success. Use the information in the report as you work through this book.

TWO

Principle 1 – Pay Yourself First

I'm excited to share my method with you, because I've witnessed so many situations where these six principles have transformed businesses and lives. Let's start with an important subject: money. Do you have enough, or are you struggling from month to month? Do you have to borrow from your business when times are hard in the hope that it won't trigger too high a tax payment when your accountant reconciles the accounts? Maybe you want to know if your business can afford to pay you an extra £20,000–£30,000 this month. Whatever the situation, are you in charge?

The principle of paying yourself first can dramatically change your business and your mindset. If you aren't already applying this principle, simply reading this chapter will shift your perspective. You might want to read it again so that the message sinks in, making notes as you go along. What is crucial is that, like everything in life, you need to act on the information to realise the benefits for your business.

The problem

When you first set up your business, you probably began with a clear intention to work less and earn more. You became more excited by the new things you were learning and the challenges you faced, and you soon became consumed by the process of developing your business. Before long, you found that you could barely keep your head above water because there was so much going on around you. You had so many different roles – you were no longer simply doing what you are an expert in. You were dealing with the administration, the marketing, customer service and legal issues, on top of building relationships with clients. You were overwhelmed, to say the least.

Alongside this, the finances have to be done. In my experience, the only financial management that a business owner does is to pay the bills and the wages. Strangely, though, even though you make sure you pay your staff, you don't pay yourself: you are always too concerned about the growing number of invoices and the level of cash in your bank account. You feel under constant pressure to create more business and generate more income, and you end up in a system of propulsion that isn't taking you anywhere. On one side, your clients are demanding a service; on the other, your suppliers are demanding payment. Your clients want to receive your product or service before they pay for it, but your suppliers are constantly telling you to pay their invoices immediately. It's hard to switch off from this.

You don't have a mechanism in your brain that allows you to withstand the pressure, so you continue to cope with it because, essentially, you still love what you do. Eventually, you work it out through trial and error... more through error, as you're too busy doing everything else in the business to stop and think of better ways to manage the situation. The result is that you invoice your customers too late and pay your suppliers too early or too late. Paying suppliers late will trigger legal issues.

What is interesting is that by paying your suppliers first, you have completely forgotten that you are an important part of the equation and you've failed to pay yourself. You believe that you are the company, and that as long as the company has money in the bank then it belongs to you. This, in fact, is not the case. It is not the company that pays your mortgage. It is not the company that pays for your petrol if you have a personal car. It is not the company that pays your food bills or your childcare fees. Although the business could do this, you don't realise it and your accountant hasn't mentioned it to you.

Does all this sound familiar? Maybe you are reading this book because you're in this situation. If that is the case, you're on the right path. Continue reading and you will cut through this vicious cycle.

The accountant's role

Your accountant may be guilty of not advising you on how to manage your business and your personal financial affairs effectively. This can be for several reasons:

- The accountant takes on a more passive role. Rather than giving you ongoing business advice, they only evaluate the situation when things go wrong.

- They see people who come to discuss their new ideas with them as potential clients, so they don't want to disappoint or irritate them. As a result, they don't challenge you about your strategies, how your business operates or the profit you have extracted.

- They treat their clients gently, so they don't want to overburden you with too much information.

- They are simply not good communicators, and don't go through many important aspects of running a business that you might need to know.

- Finally, they might not know any better. They simply *do not know enough about business to advise*.

Some business owners turn to a business coach, but it's still important to get advice from your accountant, who knows the figures and will tell you the truth. They should tell you how often your invoices should be paid, what method to use to make the payments, how to pay yourself and what to pay yourself – a salary or dividends. You need to have an honest and trusting relationship with your accountant so that they can guide and advise you. This sort of honest advice has proven pivotal for many businesses I have worked with.

Evaluating your business

This book is for the businesses that are at least three years old, are in the development stage and are ready to move to the next level. Many of them will have hit a ceiling or got stuck in a rut. They don't know what to change or where to start.

Think about how you bring up your children. Until a child is five years old, you allow them to do, to be and to build their understanding of the world. After they reach five years of age, the child is introduced to new concepts. They discover that school is about learning and not always about playing, they are given more independence, and they are introduced to the concept of money. Your business is the same: after three to five years, you need to focus on the finances.

If you're not in profit by the time your business is five years old, you need to review your position and see what assets and liabilities you have. In this context, your assets are your clients. How many do you have? Are they loyal to you? Your liabilities are your mortgage and the other personal expenses you incur. How long can you continue to pay them if your business is running out of cash?

The Elena Meskhi & Co (EMCO) ratio is a tool I have created to help you change how you think and turn your business around.

The EMCO ratio

The EMCO ratio helps you to evaluate your situation and pay yourself first.

Cost	Percentage of total turnover (£150,000–£2,500,000)
Owner's pay	30%
Admin expenses	30%
Corporation tax	10%
Salaries, including freelancers and subcontractors (human expenses)	30%

If the turnover of the business is below £150,000, the ratio is different. When your business has a turnover above £150,000, your revenue and overheads grow as you start to employ more people to help you. As you free up some of your time by employing staff, you shift your own pay ratio down to cover the increased overheads of bringing new people into your team.

EXERCISE: THE EMCO RATIO

To do this exercise, you'll need last year's financial statements, also known as your company accounts.

The table includes an example from the profit and loss account of an operating business. Fill in the two columns on the right with your own figures and ratios.

1. Use the figures in your accounts and put them into the cells provided, just as in the example. (Your sales ratio is always 100%.)

2. The ratio for salaries is an amalgamation of the amounts you pay to people involved in your business: staff, freelancers, subcontractors, virtual personal assistants and so on. Add these costs together and record them in the cell.

3. Calculate the salary ratio using the formula:

$$(C \times B) / A$$

4. Calculate the owner's pay ratio using the formula:

$$(D+E) \times B / A$$

5. Calculate the administration cost ratio using the formula:

$$(F+G) \times B / A$$

Moment of truth: what do your ratios look like?

	Example (£)	Ratio, %	Your business (£)	Ratio, %
Sales (A)		100%		
	850,000	(B)	...	...
Cost of sales				
Salaries, including social security	141,000	...	...	...
Freelancers	114,000	...	...	...
Other direct costs in relation to salaries	...	...	...	...
Total of three cells above (C)	255,000	30%	...	...
Administration costs (F)	200,000	...	...	...
Directors' remuneration (D)	9,000	...	...	...
Net profit (A-C-F-D)	386,000	...	...	...
Less corporation tax at 19% (G)	73,000	32%	...	...
Profit after tax	313,000	...	...	...
Dividends (E)	245,000	30%	...	...
Reserves	68,000	8%	...	...

Your ratios might deviate up or down, but they will give you a good idea of where you are right now.

- If your owner's pay is 20% and not 30%, you have a good structure in your business with areas for improvement. If you feel you are reaching a glass ceiling, I have a challenge for you: from this month, decide how you will improve your owner's ratio by 5% or 10%. Ways to increase your owner's ratio include increasing your sales, setting up targets, motivating the team, reconsidering suppliers and cutting additional expenses. Be mindful that this will have a knock-on effect on your expenses because there will be less money to spend.

- If your owners' pay is more than 30% (say, 50%), ask yourself whether you are working too much. Do you want to get a new person on your team?

- If you are not in profit, don't close your company yet. Keep this option in mind, though, and be sure to seek specialist advice.

- If you are in profit but instead of paying yourself 30% you're only paying yourself 5%, you've been concentrating on the business but forgetting about yourself. Maybe it's time to change.

The best outcome is for your percentages to match the ones shown in the example above. If they do, keep up the good work and use the strategies from this book to help you make your business even better.

CASE STUDY: PAY YOURSELF FIRST

A client of mine had a business turnover of about £500,000 but paid the invoices first and never paid himself. I explained that unless he changed his strategy and paid himself first, nothing would ever improve in his business. His company would continue to grow, but his expenses would creep up in line with his turnover. I advised that he change his way of thinking and start to pay himself first, but he was sceptical: 'I have bills... suppliers! They need to be paid!'

I asked him to try an experiment for a week, and he agreed. I advised that he open another bank account, move the balance from his business account into the new account, and leave all the money in that account for the full week. This left a zero balance in his business account, into which all his clients would pay their invoices. I instructed him not to pay any money out of the business account to his suppliers or creditors for the full week.

By the end of the week, the client had a chunky balance in his business account. We applied the EMCO ratio to that amount and calculated how much he had earned. I then advised that he immediately transfer 25% to his owners pay account. The client was delighted. He said he found the approach liberating and that he suddenly saw the point of running his own business. We then put aside the 20% for profit and taxes and left the remaining balance in the account. My client agreed to continue with this approach for the rest of the month. At the end of the experiment, he agreed to pay his creditors only once a month; within a short time, he had enough money to pay all his expenses and still pay himself first. He was amazed.

This client is still managing his bank account in this way. I have created a monthly management accounting system for him, which he loves. He now applies the ratio every month and keeps a record of this data. Once a month he pays a large sum into his personal bank account, and he has never looked back because this system works.

The EMCO ratio is part of the discovery. The key is to change the way you run the financial side of your business – and if you make only one change then that should be:

You start paying yourself first!

EXAMPLE: HOW TO PAY YOURSELF FIRST

The key to paying yourself first is to review the profit and loss of your business and make it a habit to pay yourself before you pay your invoices.

To do this effectively, you need to set a deadline for when to pay your suppliers; this is known as the supplier's credit terms, and different suppliers will have different timescales. By doing so, you can build up the balance in your business account, as in the case study, over a week, two weeks or a month.

Once you have received some income from your clients, you can apply the EMCO ratio. First, pay yourself and move that money to your owners pay account. Then deal with your business expenses, making sure that you have a clear understanding of the amounts, the suppliers and their due dates.

There is more on this in the chapters to come; what's important here is that you should never pay your invoices randomly. Look at a breakdown of all the outstanding invoices and their due dates. Resist any temptation to pay an invoice before the due date: it is a much better feeling to know that you have a cash balance in your account.

So, start today and pay yourself first. It will be life-changing for you and for your business, and, as I said at the beginning, nothing will change until you take action.

Summary

In this chapter we have covered the first and most vital action you need to take to turn your business around. To help you do that, I have introduced you to the EMCO ratio. If you haven't done so already, go back and apply the EMCO ratio to your business. You will be amazed by the results.

I have created a checklist to help you to nail this principle. To download it, visit www.rewire4success.com/emcoratiochecklist.

Once you've done this, you'll be ready to move on to the next chapter (Principle 2 – Stocktake) and plan your strategy for reviewing the three tiers of this principle: financial, business and personal.

THREE

Principle 2 – Stocktake

Now that you've started to pay yourself first, you're on your way to rewiring your business for success. It's vital to follow the six principles if you want to reach your business and personal goals, but you don't have to do this alone. With a good accountant supporting you, you will find that you spend less time working 'in' your business and more time working 'on' your business and towards your personal goals.

In this chapter, I will introduce you to the next of those principles: **Stocktake**. This is a key step to understanding where your business is right now. It will enable you to plan your strategy for dealing with the problems you are experiencing and moving towards your goals.

How your business evolved

Just like people do, your business goes through many stages of development. Children learn to feed themselves and then to talk; at first, they don't pay attention to other children around them. Over time, they learn to play with others and eventually they begin to learn from each other.

If you relate this to your business, you'll probably remember that set-up phase, when you were completely absorbed in getting it going. Over the first three to five years, you probably didn't take much notice of other businesses, given how immersed you were in attaining your own goals. As time passed, you probably began to notice the business network around you. This is a good time to take stock of what you have achieved so far and assess what you want for the future.

At this point, some business owners experience overwhelm and worry. They want to develop a business plan, put a strategy together and look for opportunities and partnerships around them, but they feel exhausted by the very thought and wonder where on earth they should start. They begin to feel fearful about whether their business will ever grow enough to meet the needs of their family and achieve their goals. Owning a business is an emotional roller coaster: it's a source of happiness, yet it can also cause fear and anxiety.

As the business evolves, many business owners fear that they don't have the right people in the team to deliver their product or service to the standard they want, and they worry about whether employees are following their processes correctly. Unhappy customers will damage their reputation, and these days, it's easy for people to go online and post a bad review of a service they aren't happy with.

A key fear is the financial aspect of the business. The business owner might have borrowed from friends or family to start the business. They might have taken out a bank loan or even remortgaged their house to raise cash. If the business is poorly run and doesn't generate enough money, this becomes a serious threat that cannot be ignored, as it will affect not only the business but also its employees and their families.

Many of the clients who come to me are frustrated because they are working continuously but failing to get the results they want. They feel like they are pushing a rock uphill but as soon as they get it to the top, when they should be able to relax and spend more time with their family, the rock begins to roll back down, taking them with it. They worry about financial security for themselves, their family and their employees. They end up staying at the office for longer to make more money, spending less and less time at home. The media adds to this stress by promoting news stories about interest rates, banks calling in loans, companies that have gone into liquidation because they couldn't make their payments and big tribunal cases brought by unhappy employees. As a result, some people return to the security of paid employment rather than continuing to go after their dream.

Those clients who have worked with me and applied my model have come out of the other side of this stress and anxiety. They have found a work-life balance that is suitable for them, and they have discovered how to take their business to the next level.

Hard work without strategy

Stocktake

This stage looks at three tiers: financial, business and personal.

Financial stocktake

I mentioned this in the previous chapter. Now you are ready to dive into your figures, I will go into more detail.

Profit and loss statement and balance sheet

This time you will need your profit and loss statement and your balance sheet close to hand.

First, let's look at the differences between these two reports.

Your **profit and loss statement** is the summary of your business activity for a set period, usually a year. Over a twelve-month period, you can see the total turnover (money **earned** by the business) and the business expenses

incurred during the period. These figures are in bold here to highlight that these amounts are not what you have in your bank account. According to accountancy principles, the turnover is a sum of all invoices *issued* during the period. Whether or not the payments have been received by your business does not matter for this report.

Your **balance sheet** is a snapshot of your business performance at one moment in time, usually on the last day of the financial year. It shows what the business has and what it owes to other parties. In this report I want you to look at two categories: **trade debtors** and **trade creditors**. These categories will show the amount your business should expect to receive from your customers (debtors) and the amount it should expect to pay your suppliers (creditors).

Are you still with me?

Now let's understand the figures in here. We are going to concentrate on the four categories described above and what the figures can tell us.

EXERCISE: DEBTOR AND CREDITOR DAYS

If you prefer, you can use a calculator at www.Rewire4success.com/book/calculator.

Debtor days

This is the number of days your customers take to pay your invoices. This figure must be the same as (if not lower than) the number of days shown in your terms of trade with your customers or on the platform you use to collect your funds. For example, if you take debit or credit card payments using a terminal, you might see a delay from when the client pays you to when the money arrives in your bank account, because the provider will take time to collect and transfer the funds to you.

Use the following formula to calculate your debtor days:

(Trade debtors / Sales) x 365

Creditor days

This is the number of days your business takes to pay your suppliers. Use the following formula:

(Trade creditors / Expenses (except salaries and depreciation)) x 365

Insights

The insights from this information will be different for every business, and your accountant might already have mentioned them to you. Ask yourself the following questions:

- What are your debtor days?
- What are your payment terms for your customers?
- What are your terms with the platform you use to take payments?
- Are your debtor days higher or lower than your payment terms for your customers?
- What are your creditor days?
- What are your major suppliers' payment terms?
- Are your debtor days higher or lower than your creditor days?

The answers to these questions will guide you on what direction to take. If you would like more help with this, feel free to reach out to me.

Business stocktake

When I start working with new clients, we do a Business Brainstorm 100 together. This helps the client to stop and think about what is actually going on for them and their business. I ask them to come up with 100 problems in their business, no matter how big or how small. Once they have created this long list, we can start to organise the problems and develop solutions. We boil down those 100 problems to find the main causes. These root problems are unique to each client.

Do this exercise for yourself so you can start to develop a strategy to move your business to where you want it to be. If you have not done your scorecard yet, please visit www.rewire-4success.com/book/scorecard. Once it is complete, you will receive a report with the bespoke advice for your business.

Personal stocktake

A personal stocktake is also important at this stage. Once you can understand the problems in your business, you need to identify what you actually want, not just from the business but personally. It is vital that your accountant is part of this discussion and gets a full understanding of this. Some accountants focus only on business goals, but I believe that they need to know your personal goals too. What type of house or car do you aspire to own? Do you want your children to be privately educated? Will they go to university? This, of course, connects with establishing your 'big why' for your business.

Business owners can be reluctant to share this personal information because they only want to talk to their accountant about their business. In my experience, the business should never be looked at in isolation, because the owners often allow their work to invade their personal life. This creates a connection and an interdependency between the two that runs deep. For your accountant to advise you properly, they need to get to know you and understand what is relevant for you. That's why it's so important to have a good relationship with your accountant.

If you struggle to give personal information to your accountant, think of it this way. Many businesses only manage to survive with the help of a husband, wife or partner. Sometimes, a husband or wife will do all the administration for the business – sending out invoices and chasing payments, for example. Some partners might create and update the business website or look after the social media accounts. Others might answer the phone and arrange appointments. These roles become inseparable from family life and household duties. They are key to keeping the business afloat and, more often than not, they are unpaid. That is why your personal situation is so important for tax planning. Your accountant needs to know who is involved in the business, what they do, how they contribute, if you pay them and, if so, how.

Only when you provide full information can your accountant understand where you would like to be. You might want to sell the business or grow it. Having a team will give you the freedom and confidence to go on holiday, travel the world or spend time with your family, safe in the knowledge that the business will still function and provide services while you're away. Your overall goal determines how soon you can put your plans in place. If you want to make sure that work happens efficiently in your absence, you might need to spend time building systems and processes. If you want to remove yourself from your business as soon as possible, you'll need to concentrate on expanding your team so you can begin to step back from the business.

The accountant's plan

Once your accountant has all the information from your stocktake, they can help you develop a strategy for the future. Don't forget to continue to complete the scorecard online. This will identify the weaknesses and potential threats to your business and give you a picture of where you are right now.

Your accountant should be ready to devise a plan with you so that you can begin to take your business to where you want it to be. With my clients, I agree what they want to do and what problems are a priority for them, and then we create a plan of action together.

In Chapter One we discussed the duty of a good accountant. I believe your accountant should support you in developing your plan and work with you to help you deal with the problems in the business and achieve your goals. To be able to do this, your accountant has to be up to the job. When hiring an accountant, consider these aspects:

- Purpose

- Competence

- Accountability

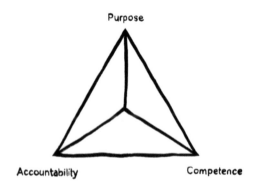

What to consider when hiring an accountant

Purpose

What do you want your accountant to do?

Before you hire an accountant, think about why you want to hire them and decide what you need them to do for you. Once you understand these things yourself, you can confidently discuss your expectations with your new accountant and give them clear information on your purpose in running a business and how you expect them to help you achieve your goals. This ensures that there is clarity between you and the accountant before you commit to hiring them.

Competence

Are they up to the job?

Hire an accountant who specialises in – and is competent in – your area of business. Treat your business in the same way as you would treat your health: if you have a general health issue then you'll probably go to your GP, but if you have a more serious problem then you will want to see a consultant or a specialist in that area. General advice is useful, but if you run a restaurant or you own a dental practice then it would be more beneficial to go to an accountant who specialises in that sector.

Be sure that they are competent in that field. Find out how many clients they have and ask for case studies showing how they have helped similar businesses in your position. Find out how respected they are among their associates. Have they been published? Do they speak at industry events? Get whatever information you need to ensure that you are confident in their skills and experience.

Accountability

How will you ensure that they work to a good standard?

How will you know if your accountant is doing a good job? Accountability is something that business owners do not pay enough attention to when it comes to the financial side of their business. As I've said before, I believe it is the accountant's duty to get to know your business and not just to appear when your tax return is due. To make sure that happens, you need to say what you want so that your accountant is clear from the start.

If you want your accountant to provide weekly, monthly or quarterly reports, what will they need from you to prepare that information? What timescales do you want to set? It's important that you can meet those deadlines yourself so your accountant can complete the reports you have asked for on time. In this way, you can agree how you will measure their work and effectiveness before you enter into a contract with them.

When I work with new clients, I agree these three parameters upfront so that I am clear on what is expected of both of us. This reduces the risk of miscommunication and problems arising from misunderstandings.

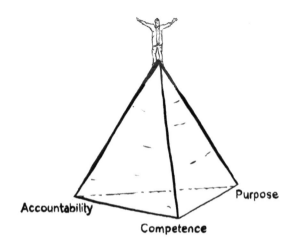

Accountability

Purpose

Competence

By ensuring all those three criteria are satisfied, your relationship will be in tip-top shape. My clients find these principles work in any relationship, not just with their accountant.

CASE STUDY: TAKING STOCK

Andrew has a six-figure business and is considered a successful business owner in his circle. He has a premium car, a house with a mortgage and a young family. He asked me to give him an independent valuation because he was thinking about selling his business. This is how the conversation went:

Andrew: You see, Elena, I've been building my business for the last five years. I've spent countless hours in the office. I think it's time to sell. I want my freedom back.

Me: That's interesting. I bet you started your business to get your freedom, and now you're saying you've got a prison instead.

Andrew: I do everything in my company from admin to marketing, even the legal work. If that's not a prison then I don't know what is. I'm tired and I want to spend time with my family.

Just by looking at the financial data for Andrew's business, I could see why he felt like he was in prison.

Me: What payment terms do you offer to your customers?

Andrew: Two weeks – fourteen days.

Me: Is there a reason, then, why your clients pay you, on average, in 69 days?

Andrew: We had a problem with the administrator in the company who was supposed to chase the payments. I didn't have time to do it myself. Maybe that's the reason.

Me: You don't seem to have any creditors. Looks impressive.

Andrew: Yes, I'm very proud of this. My accountant taught me to pay the invoices as soon as they arrive, so I never have to worry that someone will sue me.

We made a few more discoveries during that meeting about advice that Andrew's accountant had given him. I took on the work of valuing his business, and while I was doing this, I gave Andrew the task of filling in a scorecard to evaluate the position of his business.

Two days later, Andrew called me. He was euphoric, and said that he had changed his mind about selling his business and that he had had a light-bulb moment when he read my report. Thanks to the clarity provided by the report, he knew what he needed to do to get his freedom back and double his turnover.

Summary

The Stocktake principle is an essential step in rewiring your business for success. Now that you have survived the first five years, take time to complete a stocktake of where you are now by following these steps:

- Calculate your debtor and creditor days. Compare the figures with the terms you give to your customers and get from your suppliers.

- Identify the problems you are experiencing in your business. Once you have done this, you will have a clearer understanding of what's holding you back.

- Identify your personal and business goals, remembering that the two are inseparable.

- Develop an action plan with your accountant. Identify which problems you will deal with first and what actions you need to take to make improvements.

In the next chapter, we will move to the third principle – Rewire – where we will begin to plan your strategy for achieving your goals and gaining your freedom.

FOUR

Principle 3 – Rewire

The Brainstorm 100 in the previous chapter will have flagged 100 problems, big and small, that need to be resolved. The next step is to dilute all 100 problems into three leading categories. In 99% of the businesses I have worked with problems fall into the cash, systems and team categories.

These problems are often historical. For example, if a business owner didn't have time to put any terms of business together when they started their business, they might never have added a line to the invoice template that says payment is due in seven days. Because of this, they receive payments late or deliver the service before the invoice is even sent.

That's why the principle of **Rewire** is so important. In this chapter, you will learn my blueprint for dealing with these issues. If after five years of running a business you still have problems with your cash, systems and team, you've been repeating the same old patterns that lead to the same old outcomes. In other words, you have formed a habit in how you run your business. Now is the time to change it.

By following this principle, you will rewire how you do things in your business by creating a better routine. Habits are part of life: we brush our teeth morning and night, and we eat meals three times a day. Often, we are not conscious of our habits until we want to create a new one, such as doing daily exercise. It takes up to 66 days to replace an old habit with a new one, and it is only when we try to do this that we realise how difficult breaking a behaviour pattern can be.[1]

This is why I suggest that when you are implementing the principles in this book, you leave time between each one so you have room to take the actions needed to form your new habits. To reduce stress, it's best to implement the principles one by one; when one principle has become ingrained in your business, you can move on to the next. It's also important to be mindful of the other trap that business owners fall into: paralysis analysis. When you strive for perfection it can prevent you from implementing crucial changes. The draft plan that is executed is better than the perfect plan that is left on the shelf.

There are several components that, when working well, will resolve the key problems of cash, systems and team and enable your business to make money. They are:

---

1   https://blogs.ucl.ac.uk/bsh/2012/06/29/busting-the-21-days-habit-formation-myth/

- Bookkeeping platforms

- Sales

- Expenses

- Relationship with banks

- Team

Bookkeeping platforms

Before you read on: the shoebox doesn't work anymore. After five years in business, you shouldn't be using that informal and inefficient system. You need to modernise, get in line with current practice and invest in good online bookkeeping software that will suit your needs. There are at least twenty options available at the moment, so do your research on each system. They all have their pros and cons, and it's up to you as the business owner to make the right decision for you. When doing your research, pay attention to how quickly the developer adapts to changes. The rules can change as much as twice a year and with such speed that the software of your choice must be dynamic and adaptable. The top brands are Xero, Sage, QuickBooks and FreeAgent. Google will list many more, but you'll see these four systems at any business fair these days.

You might think that you can move away from shoebox accounting by introducing a simple spreadsheet. Many business owners think that this is doing their accountant a favour, but it doesn't help in any way. It only adds another layer of complexity to your accounts, because your accountant needs to check that every entry on that spreadsheet is correct. It's a waste of your time to use spreadsheets when technology is available that allows you to upload a photo of your receipt to an application that will transcribe the receipt for you. With these systems, there's no need to enter information like this on to a spreadsheet.

Another obsolete process is the employee expense report. It takes far too much time for your employees to record and report their expenses, for that information to be processed by your accountant and for the reimbursement to be released by your accountant – or, in the worst-case scenario, by you!

Another reason it's important to get an online accounting system is that HM Revenue & Customs (HMRC) has introduced the Making Tax Digital system. HMRC wants to make tax as accurate as possible and reduce delays between submission and processing, and these endeavours have been rather successful. Making Tax Digital is one step in automating the process; HMRC will continue to introduce changes to shorten timespans, and soon the only way to submit your tax return will be electronically. That's why it's vital to modernise your accounting systems now.

Sales

The most important area of business to address is your sales process. Sales equal cash; they are the nutrients that sustain your business. Regardless of how you do things now, the sales cycle for any business should be as follows:

1. Prepare a quote for the client

2. Send the quote to the client, along with your terms and conditions

3. Receive the client's acceptance of your quote and your terms and conditions

4. Send the invoice to the client, giving them as many payment options as possible

5. Receive payment from the client

6. Deliver the service

If you have any other sequence, you need to review it. Please do not send your bill after you have delivered the service; invoice for 50% at the beginning and the balance at the end. Invoicing afterwards may be how the rest of your industry operates, but I am challenging you to be a pioneer and change your terms and conditions so that your business can finally start making money. As an accountant – the person who has seen it all (or almost all) – I am going to be honest with you. If you don't change how you get paid, your business will fold.

Usually, the cycle starts with a call or a meeting with the prospect, during which you explain how you work and what you can do for them. At the end of the meeting, you give the prospect information on the product or service they are interested in and discuss anything that you need from them. You also discuss your fees per hour or per service, your termination rules and what will happen if something goes wrong. All this information is standard content for terms and conditions, but so often it is not set out in writing. If this is the case for your business, dedicate time to get your terms and conditions written down so you can give them to your clients. If you have never had terms and conditions before, now is the time to introduce them.

It is vital that you send the potential client your quote as soon as you have finished the meeting. This is when your prospect is 'hot' (as they say in marketing terms) and ready to commit to buying your services. If you don't have this process automated and the quote readily available, you may as well forget about that prospect becoming your client. If there are any delays, the client will go off the boil and won't sign your quote.

If you have clients who are already using your services but you have never sent them your terms and conditions, send them a copy now with a friendly note. This will show them that you are serious about your business, and you will find that it transforms how they view your service. They will see that you are here for the long haul and that you're not some lightweight company that will disappear overnight.

Make it as easy as possible for your prospect to accept your offer. To do this, add an 'Accept' button to the electronic copy of your terms and conditions. If you've sent them as an attachment, ask your prospect to email you back to say they have agreed. Don't overcomplicate the process: if you ask someone to print out a copy, sign it and post it back to you, it will never arrive. They will not bother to do it nowadays. They can sign with the click of a button or even, in some situations, confirm their agreement by return of email.

Once the client has accepted your quote and your terms, you should follow it up immediately with the invoice. Include a direct debit button so you can collect the payment automatically. I've seen a lot of clients who use bookkeeping software but issue their sales invoices in Word or Excel. This hybrid system implies that they have started the transformation but lost interest and are now stuck between two worlds. Please don't fall into this trap: if you invoice in that way, you're missing out on lots of features and handy tricks.

Give the client a variety of payment methods to choose from: bank transfer, PayPal, debit card and credit card. The main objective is to simplify the payment process for the client. If you have implemented the payment stage correctly, you shouldn't need to set up reminders, but sometimes clients don't pay on time and you will need to have a way of reminding them automatically. To help you with this, you can download a template for reminders from www.Rewire4success.com/book/paymentreminders.

Expenses

If 'sales' is cash coming in, 'expenses' is cash going out. All business expenses need to be recorded and the receipts kept, but HMRC no longer demand that the original is retained. This is helpful, because you can save everything electronically in Dropbox or Google Drive, but HMRC is still strict about requiring proof of expenses.

Some of my clients have told me that they couldn't provide proof of purchase because it was lost, so they decided to enter the expense as personal. Let me explain what that means: if you don't have the receipt, the expense will be allocated against the director's loan account, which means that you have spent the money personally.

EXAMPLE: BOOKKEEPING AND PERSONAL INCOME

A business owner spends £50 a month from their personal income on items related to their business, which means this income will already have been taxed. If they pay in cash and lose the receipt, there will be no record of the transaction.

That £50 a month will add up to £600 over the year. If the business owner receives that money back through their salary, the tax they will pay overall on that amount will be £495, taking account of income tax and employer's National Insurance.

I hope this example will give you the incentive to reconsider the bookkeeping process in your business.

You might not realise that your company can pay for an item you have just bought. In the next chapter, I'll discuss several types of expenses and the relevant tax rules that you might wish to explore.

Some business owners don't have a system in place for expenses, so buying happens chaotically. They buy something online but forget to print out the electronic invoice, or they buy something in a shop and shove the receipt in their bag, only for it to be lost forever. If this sounds like you, it's vital that you create a system to make your life easier and keep track of those receipts.

To keep track of receipts received via email, you can set up a filter. For example, if you have a Dropbox account, you can create an email address for it. When a receipt lands in your inbox, you can forward it to that email address and it will arrive in your Dropbox folder safe and sound. Giving your accountant access to this folder doesn't cost you anything and allows them to track your expenses. It's easy to manage paper receipts in this way too. Simply take a photo of the receipt and send it to the same Dropbox email address. If you want to use a software application, you can take the same approach: email that receipt or expense to your software and it will automatically be logged. If you use bookkeeping software, which is the gold standard, you will have an email associated with your company account and all the expenses that you forward to that email address will be processed by that software.

Choose one of these systems to implement and get into the habit of using it. Make sure your system is documented so everyone on your team who spends the company's money can follow the same process. In this way, you will finally be in control of your expenses.

I mentioned the need to keep track of expenses. Now let's talk about successful habits for paying invoices. Remember that unfortunate habit that Andrew had developed, which I mentioned in the previous chapter. Any business owner I have ever worked with has said to me, in one way or another, that they don't have enough time to get things done. From working with successful people, I know that there is no such concept as 'finding time'. Successful people operate with the concept of 'making time'.

Two key rules for paying invoices

1. **Don't pay an invoice as soon as it arrives.**
   Decide on what day you will pay your invoices, using whatever credit terms you have arranged with your suppliers. Read the supplier's invoice carefully to check if they have credit terms of fifteen, thirty, forty-five or sixty days and honour those terms, but do not pay straight after the invoice has arrived. You might be able to extend your credit terms by an extra two weeks, and you will be surprised by how much this works to your advantage. The most important thing is to pay on time: you don't want to get a reputation for always paying your bills late.

2. **Set up a system for paying your invoices.**
   Once you've received an invoice, send it to the person you have delegated to

make payments for you. They must
create a system to track the invoices,
and twice a month they should tell you
which invoices need to be paid. To start
with, choose one day a week (most likely
a Friday) when you will check and pay
the invoices. You will be surprised by
how much time you save by making this
simple change.

I advise my clients to review their expenses
every month, every quarter or at least every
six months. Over a year, you're likely to make
various decisions here and there. In January,
you might have a team member join your company and take out a mobile phone contract for
that employee. Later in the year, you might hire
another two members of staff, which means
you now need three mobile phone contracts.
If you review this situation regularly, you'll
be able to get better deals from your mobile
phone company because you have more than
one phone. Making these sorts of changes will
save your business money.

CASE STUDY: REVIEWING YOUR BUSINESS EXPENSES

A client who had lost two of their big customers told me that they wanted to protect the business by cutting down on expenses. They genuinely believed that this was the solution to the problem, and that it would keep their bottom line in a safe position. My response was 'Absolutely not!' Cutting costs would result in the total starvation of the business and make it obvious that the client was worried about losing the business. When their employees became aware of this, they would worry about their jobs, morale would sink and people would end up leaving.

I explained that a better solution would be to create a better environment for the existing clients by improving customer care and nurturing the customer relationship. This proactive approach would have a positive impact on employees and customers alike and show that the business was sustainable and was taking on new clients. The team would be happy and confident, safe in the knowledge that the company was not about to downsize and put their jobs on the line.

The moral of the story is that when you review your business expenses it's important to be vigilant about what message the resulting action might send to your team and your clients.

Banks

In my professional opinion, all businesses need at least four bank accounts to run successfully:

- Sales

- Tax and VAT

- Expenses

- Reserve

A good bank will be able to open the additional bank accounts you need quickly, without any hassle. Let me explain each account in more detail.

Sales account

As I mentioned when introducing the EMCO ratio in Chapter Two, all your invoices should be paid into your sales account. Include the account details on all your invoices and set up as many payment options as possible so it's easy for clients to pay you. These should all link to your sales account so you can monitor your cash coming in.

Keep this account safe: don't pay any expenses from it, don't set up any direct debits or standing orders and don't use a debit card. Do not reveal the account details for any other purpose than for making payments into it.

Tax and VAT account

If your business is VAT registered, the strict rule is that you must transfer 20% of VAT and 10% from net sales of the money that arrives in your sales account to your tax and VAT account.

EXAMPLE: SETTING ASIDE PAYMENT FOR TAX AND VAT

You have £1,200 in your sales account, with £1,000 being the net figure.

Of this net figure, £200 (20%) is the VAT element. Technically, this £200 is not your money, so it's important to transfer it to your tax and VAT account so you have enough reserves to pay your VAT to HMRC.

The additional 10% is the estimate for the future corporation tax your business will need to pay. After taking the expenses from the turnover, on average, the Corporation tax is going to be 10% on the sales figure.

The good news is that most of the time there will be a surplus in the tax and VAT account because 20% of VAT and 10% of the net sales figure is a cautious estimate. It's better to be safe than sorry, so it's a good idea to budget in such a way that as soon as a sale arrives in your account, you transfer 10% from your net sales figure.

Expenses account

Having an expenses account makes it easier to log the expenses that your business incurs. You should pay all your business expenses from this account. In line with the EMCO ratio, you should transfer 30% of the money you receive in your sales account to your expenses account. You then pay your direct debits and standing orders from the expenses account. Remember, don't pay anything direct from your sales account; everything that needs to be paid should come from the expenses account. That means you will need a debit card for this account, but not for your sales account.

Reserve account

Your reserve account is where you keep the profit that your business generates. In line with the EMCO ratio, you should transfer 30% of your sales amount into your reserve account. Remember, this ratio might change depending on which tier your business is in and the turnover it generates (see Chapter Two).

Relationship with banks

I divide banks into two categories: high-street banks and online banks.

High-street banks

These are reputable banks with a long history, many of which have been in existence for hundreds of years. Behind that history is a legacy of infrastructure that affects the way that the banks work. They don't have the luxury of using new platforms because they make millions of transactions using an age-old system which they have to run continuously. Because of this, processes can be slow and less user-friendly. Because high-street banks are reputable, it might be a good idea to place your sales account and reserve account with them.

Online bank accounts

Online banking is easy and fast. These banks are more adaptable than high-street banks. You can open a bank account in twenty minutes and get your debit card within two days. You will be up and running quickly and you can also add your PA, your accountant or your office manager to the account if you're happy to delegate financial roles to others. They can then make payments on your behalf so you don't have to get involved with paying invoices and the related administrative tasks. I would advise that your expense and tax accounts are both with online banks, as you will use these accounts regularly.

Team

Your team includes all the people who are involved in building your business. They can be employees or freelancers, and they include people you would expect to play a part in your business, such as solicitors, accountants and IT providers. You might want to stop at this point and make a list of all the categories of people you have involved in your business. You may be surprised by how many people you engage with to help run and grow your company.

EXERCISE: WHO IS MY BUSINESS?

Make a cup of tea, turn off your phone and get some paper and a pen. Think about the people involved in all areas of your business. Make a list:

- you
- your personal assistant
- sales manager
- receptionist
- solicitor
- marketing manager/agency
- HR consultant
- business coach
- cleaner

Continue adding to the list until you exhaust it.

Keep this list as we will use it in the next exercise.

It's important that each person in your team has your terms and conditions of working with your business so that they are clear about their responsibilities and what is expected of them. For employees, that should be a contract of services; for freelancers, it should be a contract for service. As an employer, it is your legal duty to provide every employee with their terms of employment within two months of their start date. If this doesn't happen, the employee can take you to an employment tribunal and sue you for compensation. This is serious and will leave a bitter taste in your mouth, as the person will still be working for your company.

It is important that freelancers sign contracts, especially if they contribute to the creativity of your business; for example, by doing copywriting, web design and development or picture design. Their contract for service should specify that the freelancer does not have any right to the product once it has been created. Otherwise, you have no legal right to claim that whatever they have produced is yours.

If you need help with drafting a contract, you can download templates for freelancer and employee contracts from www. Rewire4success.com/book/team. You will also receive a checklist of what you need to ask employees and freelancers to provide when you start working with them.

EXERCISE: WHO DOES WHAT?

Take another sheet of paper and divide it into five columns:

- Operational
- Marketing
- Legal
- Human resources
- Financial

Using the list of people from the previous exercise, assign each to a column.

Once complete, answer the following questions:

- Do you create the vision for your business?
- Do you write blogs or posts in social media or articles?
- Have you put yourself in the Marketing column?
- Do you work with each client on their projects or provide them services?
- Have you put yourself in the Operating column?

- If you sign a contract in relation to your business, do you review it yourself?
- Have you put yourself in the Legal column?
- Do you interview prospective employees in your company?
- Are you the point of contact if your employees have a problem?
- Have you put yourself into the HR column?
- Do you pay your suppliers? Do you keep track of your expenses and business expenses?
- Have you put yourself into the Financial column?

The point I'm trying to make is that you are a very important person within your business.

As the director of the company, you also need to have a contract that sets out your duties to the company. There is more about this in Chapter Six when we discuss your tax optimisation strategy, but at this stage it's simply necessary to mention that you need a contract because you are part of the team.

There is a misconception that you need a solicitor to advise you on employee and freelancer contracts. As this is part of the accounting and financial life of the company, your accountant should be capable of providing advice.

Summary

In this chapter, we have covered the key solutions to the problems associated with cash, systems and team in your business. These include:

- Introducing an online bookkeeping system, and getting rid of shoeboxes and spreadsheets

- Creating payment terms and conditions

- Implementing easy payment methods for your prospects

- Not paying your invoices as soon as they arrive, but making sure you pay them on time

- Setting up a system that consolidates payments into one day each week, fortnight or month

- Opening four bank accounts – sales, expenses, tax and VAT, and reserve – to apply the EMCO ratio

- Ensuring all your employees, freelancers and you as director are issued with contracts

If you have not completed your business score-card to identify the weaknesses in your business, you can do so at www.Rewire4success.com/book/scorecard.

Now let's move on to Principle 4 – Automate – to discover how to streamline your processes and what tools will help you do this.

FIVE

Principle 4 – Automate

Why automate?

After completing the exercise in the previous chapter and realising just how important you are to your business, I hope you have not lost your motivation to get your freedom back. Some of my clients during that exercise exclaim, 'I had no idea that I'm doing all that!' This is the part when you will begin see the light at the end of the tunnel as we discuss how to get rid of many tasks you have been doing for years.

Automation is another method of delegation. When we automate a process, we delegate the task to artificial intelligence. In other words, we delegate the task to the software we have chosen to use, which will automatically do the task for us.

Many businesses that I have worked with share the following problem. The business owner, by nature, is a perfectionist with an 'I can do it' attitude, but this doesn't sit well with the fact that they have hundreds of responsibilities. They have goals, tasks and meetings and they are constantly being distracted. Perfectionism in a business owner can lead to that person doing everything themselves. Often, because they are so busy, they move tasks like collecting receipts and paying invoices to the bottom of their to-do list, and they become a bottleneck. This is a project management term meaning that one section with limited capacity becomes the limiting factor for the whole process.

Because perfectionists think they are the only ones who can do a good job, it becomes difficult for them to delegate. Don't postpone this: when it comes to the accounting side of your business, you need to do this now. In my experience, business owners tend to find it easier to delegate tasks to artificial intelligence than to real people. I have learned how to streamline business accountancy processes in such a way that business owners can do so with ease themselves.

Once you have started using the tools suggested in this chapter, you will never get another email from your accountant asking for more information so they can complete your accounts. The tasks around you will get done without you having to be involved. Wouldn't that be a dream come true?

That's why this principle of automation is so important. If all you are doing now is chasing your tail – delivering services, arranging appointments, invoicing clients, paying expenses and doing your own bookkeeping and accounting – then you are wasting time that you could be spending on building your business. Automation is the only solution that will give you back this precious time.

First, you need to evaluate the problem and formulate solutions. To use an analogy, if you want to get into the habit of going to the gym, you don't decide that for thirty days you'll wake up every morning and put on your training gear, for the next thirty days you'll put on your gear and get into the car, and for the last thirty days you'll drive to the gym. You get on and do it, moving from your home to the gym in the quickest possible way.

The same applies to automating your processes. As I mentioned in Chapter Four, many businesses move from keeping their receipts in a shoebox to putting them on a spreadsheet. They wait until they've refined that process before they decide to delegate this to their accountant or start using online software. They think that they are moving forward with this step-by-step approach, but in fact it is only creating delays in their business growth. That's why you need to find the shortest distance possible to progress from A to B, avoiding any unnecessary steps.

The accountant's role

The good news is that your accountant is there to help you automate your processes, so as long as they are competent and reputable you will be in safe hands. You will need to specify exactly what you want and why. With this information, a good accountant will advise you on what you need to do and how to do it. They should know each accounting package inside out, and they will at least know the packages they work with.

You might think that it will be expensive to involve your accountant but consider the hours you are currently spending on entering receipts into your spreadsheet. This is the amount of time you will free up if you automate your processes and delegate this work to your accountant. Given their expertise in bookkeeping and accounting software, it will take them less time than it takes you to process your receipts. When you're doing things that are outside your area of expertise and not your passion, those things will take longer; and by saying 'yes' to doing those boring tasks you're saying 'no' to delivering your service to your clients – the thing that you love to do.

The principle of Automate falls in line with the principle of Rewire. Consider automating any business process that is easy and repetitive. Let's start by looking at how automation works in the key areas of your business – sales, expenses, your relationship with your bank and your team.

Sales

Your sales process repeats itself every month, and sending out invoices is one task that can be automated easily. Through automation, an invoice can be issued on a particular day, at an exact time, in a specific format with exactly the same payment terms. It also removes human error from the process. You may be invoicing more than fifty clients at a time, so there's a chance of something being forgotten or a name or address being mixed up. Reminders are sent to clients automatically, and once the payment has been received the invoice is marked as paid. Your client will be notified at every stage of the process. Through automated invoicing, clients can use a credit card or a debit card, make an electronic payment or use a cryptocurrency. There's more on this in the section on your relationship with banks.

If you've automated the full process, you won't need to get involved in any aspect of invoicing. You only need to be involved at the first stage when you send a quote to the client. More on that later in this chapter.

CASE STUDY: AUTOMATING SALES SYSTEMS

I worked with a medical practice that optimised their use of automation. Before automation, patients sometimes did not turn up for their appointments, which meant that the practice lost money and valuable time. When patients did attend, their payments were taken by the receptionist and a new appointment was made if necessary.

I looked at their processes and helped them implement a different approach. First, they set up an online booking system, which patients could access easily via the practice website. Alongside that, they introduced a way of taking payments for appointments electronically. Crucial to the success of this system was the cancellation policy. On booking, patients received an automatic notification that a 48-hour cancellation policy was in operation and that the patient's fees would not be refunded if they cancelled within this period.

Once the full system had been implemented, the practice found that the number of 'no shows' greatly reduced. There was less administration involved in taking payments after appointments, freeing up the practice time to concentrate on the customer experience instead. The administrator now spent less time on the phone because patients were happy to book online: it gave them the flexibility to book the time they wanted and they could use the booking system day or night. The number of errors in patients' data were also reduced, as the patients entered their details themselves.

Implementing a system like this will free you up to spend more time concentrating on your business and its strategic needs rather than training staff, chasing payments and the other routine tasks that surround sales.

Relationship with banks

If your accountant has one anxiety, it is about missing pages from your bank statements. In almost all cases, this happens when a business owner has another savings account which has a tiny balance in it. They might have forgotten about that account because they never use it, but their accountant still needs to see the statement. In another situation, a business owner might have ten bank accounts, and the accountant will need to see statements for all of them.

Your accountant needs to ensure that all the information provided is accurate. If you have automated the bank relationship process and arranged for your accountant to receive your bank statements as quickly as possible and in full, you won't have to waste time looking for missing information. For this to happen, your bank accounts need to be connected to your accounting software.

Your statements won't include details about cheque payments, which your accountant will also need to see – but in my view, businesses should no longer be making payments by cheque. A bank transfer is a faster and more secure method of payment. If you do make a cheque payment, send an email to yourself or your accountant with the cheque number and a description. On so many occasions, my clients have lost their cheque stubs and they have no other record of why they wrote the cheque. If you ask the bank for a copy of the cheque, they will charge you for this service.

Don't use cash to pay expenses or accept cash payments from clients, because you cannot trace these transactions. If you receive cash from a client and you don't log it, your accountant won't know what the payment was for. They will assume that the client still owes you money, because the invoice is still marked as unpaid on the system. The same applies to cash payments for expenses. If you pay for an item with cash and then lose the receipt, there is no way of proving that you really did buy that item. In short, don't use cash in your business dealings; use a bank transfer instead.

If your bank isn't able to connect your bank accounts with your accounting software, transfer your accounts to a bank that does provide such services (read the information on different bank accounts in Chapter Four). If they say that they won't connect your accounts in the interest of security issues, you are in a secure but unhelpful bank for your business. Keep the secure bank account to use as your reserve account, as you won't be using that on a day-to-day basis. For successful automation, the accounts that you use to receive payments and pay expenses have to be user-friendly. There's more detail about this in the Expenses section of this chapter.

If you are a business owner with a turnover of between £150,000 and £2,500,000, I'm sure you have enough on your plate without having to think about buying stamps and stationery. On the other hand, I also understand that sometimes you don't want to give team members access to your bank accounts. To overcome this problem, you can set up a bank account with a smaller revenue and give access to your office manager or personal assistant so they can make payments on your behalf. This will take the pressure off you by giving you more time and reducing the amount of administration you have to do.

Expenses

You will need to create a system for recording expense receipts regularly and routinely. The whole team will need to know this process and follow it strictly. If someone has the authori-sation to buy something for the company and you need to reimburse them, you'll need another process for this so there are no misun-derstandings. Employees should have to pro-duce a receipt for an expense before they are paid for it. If people complain, you can always defer to your accountant and say that it is their rule, not yours. As long as the process is fol-lowed, your accountant won't mind.

If your accountant has to spend extra time sort-ing out your business expenses, you will have to pay more for this. The chances are that it will be because something has gone missing. The amount can't be written off as an expense because there is no receipt for it, so you will end up paying tax on it. It's as simple as that. With all these reasons to automate your expenses, how can you not want to do it right now?

Another business expense is mileage. There is a misconception that if you use your per-sonal car for your own travel, you can present receipts for fuel as business expenses. But this is not how tax works: you can only claim for mileage related to business travel, and the tax office insists that you declare your business mileage. For the mileage that you can claim, you will get 45p per mile. If you consider that you might do 10,000 miles per year, £4,500 is a substantial sum of money in the form of additional expenses in your company accounts. I know many business owners don't like to keep records for their mileage, but even if you only record it in a notebook that you keep in the glove compartment, you need the information to be accurate if you want to be compensated for your business travel.

If you have a business car then the car belongs to the business, which will pay for fuel, servicing and MOTs and all other overheads associated with it. You still need to record your mileage, because occasionally you or your employees might use the car for personal reasons. With modern technology, you can automate this process too.

Remember, expenses need to be paid on a certain day of the month or week. This process needs to be automated to ensure it is effective.

A good way to automate your expenses is for your accountant to prepare a report on unpaid expenses and their due dates at the end of each month so that you can decide which ones to authorise for payment.

TOP TIPS FOR AUTOMATING EXPENSES EFFICIENTLY

1. **Set up a filter on emails.** If you use Gmail, you can set up a filter so that any emails with an invoice attached go directly to your accountant, your manager or whoever is dealing with recording your business expenses.

2. **Install an app on your mobile phone to track your expenses.** Make sure all team members who are authorised to buy things for your business also download the app to their phones. If you don't want them to use an app, they should at least take a photo of their receipt on their phone and send it to the dedicated email address or bookkeeping software so it can be logged automatically.

3. **Make sure all your staff know how to use your accounting software.** If you're too busy to upload your receipts, you can delegate this to your employees. Ideally you should delegate it to your employees if you want your freedom back.

4. **Install an app on your business mobile phones to track your whereabouts and log mileage.** Get your employees to do this too. Once a week, review the app and mark the journeys that were business-related (record why) and not business-related. This will replace your mileage book.

Team

Your team needs to work smarter, not harder. To make this happen, any process that can be automated should be automated. Those processes can then be delegated to the team, giving you more time to work on high-profile tasks. By automating tasks that are part of those processes, you will also free up members of the team. For example, rather than giving your receipts to your personal assistant to scan or post to your accountant, automate the system so that your personal assistant can spend more time drafting contracts or building relationships with clients. There is no such thing as too much automation.

Automation in the team is a process of development. It is important that you and your

team continuously review the automated processes, research whether better technology is
available and update the technology you are
currently using if it becomes obsolete. Don't
ignore this: stop using the obsolete technology and switch to a newer and more beneficial option if you need to. Don't be sentimental
about the systems you've set up; embrace new
and updated software if it can help you get to
your destination faster. In the end, this will
save you and your team time and effort as you
move your business to a higher level.

This is an exercise to help you to identify
what area of your business you are ready to
automate.

EXERCISE: TIME TO AUTOMATE

You need an hour of undisturbed time, ten
sheets of paper, a pen but no cup of tea as it
would be a distraction for this exercise.

Set a stopwatch for an hour.

List all the tasks you have in your head:
review the job, reply to the email of Mr X,

pick up dry cleaning. Literally everything you might have in your head: business, personal, shopping, something to buy, anything that comes up, write your will, service the car, upgrade your mobile phone, anything.

Keep writing for thirty minutes. Do not stop for any reason.

After thirty minutes, take a clean sheet of paper and divide it into four parts as in the Eisenhower Matrix (also referred to as 'Urgent-Important Matrix'). Label each quadrant as shown.

	Urgent	Not urgent
Important	**DO** Important and urgent	**SCHEDULE** Important but not urgent
Not important	**DELEGATE** Not important but urgent	**DELETE** Not important and not urgent

Eisenhower Matrix

Now sort all your tasks in accordance with
how urgent or important they are and write
them in the appropriate quadrant.

What is in the lower left quadrant called
'Delegate'?

How would you delegate those tasks?

Summary

Automation is closely connected with the
principle of Rewire, so read that chapter again
if you need to refresh your memory. Then
assess your business and list all the processes
you can begin to automate. Work closely with
your accountant, who will be able to help you
with this.

The key processes to consider are:

- Invoicing clients

- Sending payment reminders

- Feeding business banking data into
  bookkeeping software

- Paying invoices

- Reimbursing employees' expenses

In the next chapter, we will look at Principle 5 – Optimise. You will learn how you and your accountant can work together to make the most of the improvements you have made in your business.

SIX

Principle 5 – Optimise

Principle 5 is about optimising your business, and it is at this stage that you can get the most value from working with your accountant.

In theory, you could have followed the first four principles without involving your accountant. As mentioned in Principle 4, though, delegation is important. By delegating the actions set out in the previous chapters to your accountant, you will find that they are completed faster than if you did the work yourself. You will also ensure that your processes are not duplicated and that you are introducing technology for the benefit of the business, not for technology's sake. Your accountant will be able to take an objective view on whether you have automated as much as possible, without duplication and in the simplest way. They won't be subjective or emotional about the changes you are making.

The principles in this book are for business owners who want to take action, and your accountant can help you to do this in the quickest and most effective way. You should involve your accountant in discussions about how you see your business model, how you see your brand and what results you want to achieve. Then you can engage them to make the necessary changes for you in line with an agreed strategy and timeframe.

There are many options here, and one size does not fit all. Whatever your strategy, it's important to have an optimised structure that gives you real-time information about the business:

your monthly turnover, your expenses and other crucial financial information. That real-time information is important whenever you make a business decision; for example, about buying a new computer, upgrading your software or hiring a new employee. It enables your accountant to look at the figures and give you an objective opinion on whether your plans are worth pursuing.

EXAMPLE: HIRING A NEW TEAM MEMBER

You are considering whether or not to hire a new team member. To be able to employ someone new, you'll need to generate more revenue so you can pay their salary. That means you should make your decision on the basis of sound financial data, rather than allowing yourself to be swayed by other members of staff who tell you that they're far too busy.

You need to be sure that the decision will benefit the business. Recruiting new people can actually make more work for you and the rest of the team, because each new team member requires attention, training, and time to get to know systems and clients while they get up to speed.

To make an effective decision will require analysis, and this is where your accountant can be a huge asset. They can tell you whether you have the financial resources to employ someone else and advise you on how you can make it happen.

In my experience, business owners don't often ask their accountant for advice of this sort. They usually make the decision themselves, under pressure from their team. Remember the three issues we discussed in Chapter One – cash, systems and team. When making any decision about hiring a new team member, these are the aspects you need to consider. Do you have the cash? Are your systems water-tight? If not, don't hire.

This principle of optimisation will help you use real-time data to maximise all aspects of your business: tax, finances, strategy and recruitment. By having that information to hand, you can make the right decisions for your business.

'I want to pay less tax'

When my clients say 'I want to pay less tax', my standard reply is 'How much less?' Your accountant needs to have real-time information about the financial position of your business to be able to work out what its net profit is. This makes it possible for them to see what you can optimise; for example, what your company's expenses are and whether those expenses can be offset. It allows them to analyse how much tax your business has paid in the past, and how much it will need to pay in the near future.

It's the same as deciding that you want to run a 10-kilometre race. You can book an appointment with a personal trainer and tell them you want to run faster. The question you will be asked is 'Faster than what?' It's likely that you have no idea. Unless you have records about your current running speed, how can your trainer help you achieve your goal? That's why it's so important to get the most up-to-date information about your business. Once that data is freely available in an electronic format, your accountant can interpret it whenever you need to make a decision, and any financial decision you want to make will flow faster. It's a simple matter of arranging a phone call or meeting with your accountant and giving them some homework to do. You won't have to wait for months to make a decision on how much money you can extract from the business. You can decide to recruit more staff, buy new laptops or equipment with ease and speed.

Rather than telling your accountant that you want to pay less tax, a better concern to raise is 'How much can I save and reinvest to grow my business?' Many businesses that have been running for three to five years have gone through a stage where they are just about breaking even. They then set new goals to make progress and become more stable. They explore new markets, different client needs and different products. To do this effectively, you must have the most up-to-date information available: you can't take a gamble on key decisions like this without it. The beauty of having your financial affairs up to date and available for interpretation at any time is that:

- Analysis can be done much quicker. If you need to provide the reports for banks or investors it's much faster to do. You will create a good first impression that you are in control of your business.

- You can make decisions based on how your business is performing at that moment.

When your business data is up to date and there is historic data available, you can have that conversation about tax optimisation. With that information to hand, your accountant can see the level of spending and income and give you professional advice. How the Optimise stage works will be different for every business, but in this chapter we'll look at some examples.

TOP TIPS FOR THE DIRECTOR'S CONTRACT AND EMPLOYEES WITH MULTIPLE ROLES

The importance of the director's contract, including the variety of roles this may cover, has already been mentioned. However, these duties do not imply that you must provide such services to your company. If you are good at it and you can develop, for example, the marketing campaign, then it's a benefit to the company but not your duty. What I am getting at here is that a director's salary is usually paid for doing the duties of a director. Any other services you can provide to your company as a freelancer should be paid according to a different contract that covers these services. Yes, you can work with your company in more than one capacity: as a director, for which you are paid a salary, and as a freelance marketing advisor, for which you get paid separately as self-employed on presentation of an invoice. This applies as long as you can demonstrate that services you provide are independent from each other. If you are unable to do so, you will need to outsource it instead.

EXAMPLE: INCREASING SALES

Let me share an example with you. The following table shows the current situation for a particular business:

	Current situation (£)
Sales	1,000,000
Expenses	(800,000)
Net profit before tax	200,000
Corporation tax @19%	(38,000)
Net profit after tax	162,000

If the business owner's priority is simply to boost sales, what happens to those figures?

	Current situation	Expenditure in an attempt to increase sales	Difference
	£	£	
Sales	1,000,000	1,100,000	
Expenses	(800,000)	(882,000)	
Net profit before tax	200,000	218,000	
Corporation tax @19%	(38,000)	(41,420)	
Net profit after tax	162,000	176,580	14,580

1. In an attempt to increase sales, the business owner invests 5% of their revenue into more marketing. As a result, their expenses increase by £50,000.

2. With a good marketing strategy, that will give rise to a 10% increase in sales.

3. One can assume that when the sales go up, the admin expenses also increase. This might not

    be by a huge amount: in our example, let's say they rise by 4% (£32,000).

4. What is the end result? Increasing sales by 10% led to an increase of just £14,580 in net profit after tax.

This example doesn't even begin to consider the stress connected with this strategy or the amount of extra work the business owner would have to do. They would need to monitor the marketing campaign, liaise with the marketing manager, control the customer experience so that standards don't slide and ensure that the team delivers – all at the same time as running the project.

To me, it looks like this business owner has become a busier fool. I don't doubt that they need to grow their sales, but there are smarter ways to use the financial data to earn a much higher net profit and maintain a balance between work and life. Let me share these ideas with you.

Horizon-scanning for opportunities

When your business has been running for at least three years, you'll probably have started to identify the niche you want to work in. Now that you've built up some experience, you'll have developed the mindset that allows you to spot opportunities in the market. Once you have optimised your financial information, you can look around to see what your competitors are doing, analyse data to compare your business with others and see what you need to do to improve. Opening up to the opportunities that are available is another way of optimising your business. When you have the right data at your fingertips, you'll finally be in the driver's seat.

This is the moment to review the following:

1. Price list

2. Client list

3. Services list

1. Price list

I am always shocked when I see that a business does not review its price list on a regular basis. In these cases, the business owner usually hasn't noticed that their prices are still the same as they were when they set up the business at least three years ago. How can you manage to run a business at all when the prices are like that?

Consequently, you need to review your price list every year. If you haven't looked at your price list in the last five years then you'll need a strategy for putting in place your new, higher prices. Once you've established the strategy, you'll have a script and a mental readiness and this will be easy to do.

Choose the quietest period in your business for your yearly price review. No matter what type of service you provide there will be moments when your clients are less active, whether it's the school holidays or the New Year. When your team has a bit more time, this is your opportunity to do your review.

People often ask me by how much they should increase their prices. This depends on whether you're increasing them for the first time in a few years or you put them up regularly. If it's an annual increase, I suggest that you raise your prices by 4% or 5%, in line with inflation. If it's the first increase in three to five years, you'll need to research the market and set your new prices in line with those that are above the average.

The table below shows what happens to your figures if you increase your prices by 5%:

	£	Annual 5% increase (£)	Difference (£)
Sales	1,000,000	1,050,000	50,000
Expenses	(800,000)	(800,000)	0
Net profit before tax	200,000	250,000	50,000
Corporation tax @19%	(38,000)	(47,500)	(9,500)
Net profit after tax	162,000	202,500	40,500

By raising your prices, you have improved your bottom line by £40,500 without any extra hassle.

2. Client list

We've all been there. I've started several businesses in my life, so I know the feeling of having no clients and the worry that this can cause. Then there's the excitement when you sign up a new client. Eventually, you get used to that feeling and by the time you have more than 100 clients on your books you don't get such a buzz out of it. Once you're three to five years down the line, you need to grade your clients if you haven't done so already. I use a straightforward matrix: A, G, D.

A – Amazing clients. These are the clients you like to work with. They're a pleasure to talk to, they pay on time and they use and benefit from your services.

G – Good clients. Clients in this category are similar to those in category A, but occasionally

working with them might be more compli-
cated, they like to talk too much or they pay
a little late.

D – Dead clients. These are the clients you have
no joy in working with. They always complain
about the prices, they pay late and they upset
your team – perhaps to such a degree that you
are the only person who will deal with them.

Sounds fun? Here is an exercise to look at this.
Using Excel or Google Sheets will make this
easier.

EXERCISE: ANALYSING CLIENTS

1. Download a list of your clients in
   alphabetical order into a spreadsheet.

2. The first column should be their names.

3. In the next column grade each client
   based on the 'A, G, D' matrix explained
   above.

4. Call the next three columns A, G and D.
   Now indicate in the relevant cell the annual
   retainer you receive from each client. Add
   the total of each class.

Client name	Grade	A	G	D
Mr Happy	A	10,000		
Mrs Demanding	G		7,000	
Miss You Owe Me Success	D			4,000
Total		10,000	7,000	4,000

What are your findings?

Once you have done the exercise above, set up a strategy for getting more clients in category A and no clients in category D. By doing this easy task, you will achieve two big targets:

1. You will free up your time and that of your team, especially if you've been having to work with clients who others in your team refuse to deal with.

2. You will increase your business's average price per client by getting rid of clients who were complaining about your prices and were probably paying less than your better clients.

3. Service list

It's better to do one thing a thousand times than a thousand things once. This is no-brainer if you're doing the things you love: by doing them repeatedly you become better at them and you can then charge more. By performing your service at the top level, you'll receive higher praise and better referrals.

I get it: it takes courage to stop providing services that aren't in high demand. The best way to do this is to reframe your thoughts. Rather than thinking that you're missing out by not providing the full range of services, focus on the extra time you'll be able to spend on providing better quality services for your clients. You'll be able to enhance and develop those services so that you become the go-to specialist in that niche.

The accountant's contribution

Your accountant will interpret your financial information to guide you in your decision-making. The beauty of this is that as an outsourced service, your accountant will have a more objective view of your business. They can stand back, analyse the dry data and advise you on whether a team member is profitable or not and if they are meeting their targets. They are not emotionally involved in your business, so they can be impartial when giving you advice, including on how to make those elusive tax savings. With that guidance you will pay less tax and, more importantly, you will keep more profit.

Your accountant can also guide you on using your company structure wisely so that you can be confident about what you can and cannot do and how much money you can pay yourself. For example, some business owners want to introduce target-driven bonuses to motivate staff, but they aren't sure where to start. I will repeat myself – your company's financial data is the point at which to start. Unfortunately, many profit-sharing ratio agreements in businesses are not fit for purpose.

CASE STUDY: PROFIT-SHARING RATIO

A client of mine set up a structure for their business that included freelancers. The business owner had in mind that the industry average was a 50:50 split of whatever the company was paid by its clients, but my calculations found that it was impossible to go by that average. The industry had moved away from this ratio and was using completely different share split percentages, and businesses that are three to five years old still tend to have high overheads.

In my client's case, the daily average business overheads per freelancer was £500. For the client to break even when using the 50:50 ratio, every freelancer would have to generate double the overheads: at least £1,000. Think about that for a moment. Do you have similar overheads? Every time a freelancer brought in anything less than £1,000, my client made a loss.

The freelancers were happy with this arrangement because they weren't incurring additional expenses; they simply earned 50% of whatever they made. The business owner appeared to make money because he received the other 50%, but this was an illusion: they still needed to pay the overheads. The situation was disguised further because the client had engaged several freelancers while working on generating income himself. Because the business was generating money, he didn't feel the inequity of the ratio.

When I analysed this business model on that granular level – freelancer by freelancer – it was astonishing. My client realised that over the course of the year, he had paid a freelancer over £15,000 from his own income. The freelancers were not bringing enough income into the business to use the 50:50 ratio that he had chosen. In contrast, the freelancers felt relaxed because no matter what happened they would always earn 50%. Armed with this information, my client was finally in a position to make the appropriate decisions: to set appropriate targets, change the ratios and concentrate on the strategic planning rather than working his pants off to pay relaxed freelancers.

Not surprisingly, business owners who don't have the information described in this case study are always under pressure, have to work more in the operational side of their business and need to work double-time to generate more clients.

Summary

This chapter has covered Principle 5 on opti- mising your business. The key aspects of opti- misation are:

- The importance of delegating this work to your accountant to prevent duplication and ensure all processes are optimised successfully

- It's not how much tax you pay, it's how much you can save in your business that matters

- Being open to new opportunities will increase your sales and bring you more of the right type of clients

With these points in mind, think about the actions you are going to take to optimise your business. Make a list and start working through it today.

If you have any challenges in optimising your business that you would like to discuss further, please get in touch with us. We would be happy to discuss options with you and help you prioritise which processes to optimise first.

The next chapter covers the final principle – Protect. You will find out how to protect yourself and your business from employees, accountants, HMRC and fraudsters.

SEVEN

Principle 6 – Protect

Now you have implemented the first five principles of this model, it is time to evaluate what in your business needs to be protected. This brings us to the sixth and final principle: **Protect**.

A loss-making business can be liquidated on one day and a new business opened on the next, but the profitable business, with its higher turnover and higher net profit, has much more to lose. With a profitable business, you have to both protect what you currently have and work out how to multiply your profit so your business doesn't lose value. With a bigger profit and a larger audience, you and your business might be under the spotlight, attracting extra attention from the tax office, competitors and fraudsters.

In this chapter, I will explain how you can protect yourself and your business so you can continue to focus on growing the company rather than getting caught up in stressful situations. The information in this chapter will give you guidance and food for thought, but it does not provide financial advice.

There are two aspects to protect in your business:

1. The business owner

2. The business

Protection for the business owner

As the business owner, it is essential that you are protected. You are the most important person in your business: you have the ideas and the vision, the intellectual property and the relationship with your customers and suppliers. With that in mind, you need to have insurance in case you are unable to work for some reason.

Relevant life policy

Instead of setting up a personal life policy, you can get one through your limited company. This is more tax-efficient for you; the tax savings can save you up to 50% in costs. A life policy is not the same as life insurance: life insurance is a personal expense so you must pay for it yourself, but a life policy is a business expense because it protects you as a business asset.

Executive income protection

An executive income protection policy pays an income to the business for your benefit as the director if you are no longer able to work due to long-term incapacities, such as an illness or the effects of an accident. The policy can cover up to 80% of your salary, your dividends and even your pension contributions.

Key person protection

In some businesses, losing particular people – including the owner – could significantly hinder the company's continued success. This insurance pays a sum to the business to cover loss of earnings and to help financially with finding a replacement if a key person dies or becomes incapacitated in the long term.

Protection for the business

In my work with clients I have identified four risks that business owners need to be aware of:

- Employees

- Accountants

- HMRC

- Fraudsters

Taking each one in turn, I will explain the risks and how to protect your business.

Employees

I was raving about the benefits of having a team a few chapters ago, but it's important to expose the other side of the coin: by employing people, you are taking on extra responsibilities. The team you're creating is like a family, and you are legally responsible for your employees when they're at work. With that in mind, you need to take care of them, regardless of any difficulties you may have with them. You should make the recruitment process as long and as hard as possible so you can evaluate potential candidates fully, begin to understand them and ensure that they're a good fit for your business.

Employment law favours the employee over the employer, so it's vital to take the time to get to know your applicants before they are recruited. Bringing the wrong person on board will create misery in the team, damaging morale and even damaging the business. That person will become a liability.

Unfortunately, the longer the wrong person works for a business, the harder it is to get rid of them. This can be devastating for the team when they think of all of the time that has gone into training that person and how much investment they have made with so little in return.

TOP TIPS FOR RECRUITING THE RIGHT EMPLOYEES

1. **Values matter**, especially when recruiting new members to your team. When you know what your business's key values are, you can make sure that they are matched by the values of potential employees. If you value honesty and freedom, your employees need to embrace those values too. Don't compromise on this: checking that applicants' values match will

protect your business and reduce the risk of hiring someone who could damage that business.

2. **Be aware of your legal obligations to your employees.** If you don't know what these are, your accountant can guide you. As mentioned earlier, you need to give each employee a written statement of their employment particulars within two months of the date they start working for you. If you don't follow this rule, the employee can bring you to an employment tribunal and claim up to four weeks' salary as compensation. When the tribunal is over, that person will still be in your employment – imagine how damaging this will be to the morale in your business. To avoid difficult situations like this, familiarise yourself with what you need to do by law and follow it through to the end.

3. **Get the legal paperwork right.** Mistakes will be costly and there is no excuse for making errors when you can easily check the information online or better still, with your accountant. As the director of your company, you are responsible for getting this right.

4. **If an employee doesn't fit, follow the process for dismissing them.** Your dismissal procedures

should be part of your employee handbook. Remember, you can't get rid of someone just because you don't like them or they don't fit the job specification: you hired them, and if they've got through their probation period you've had enough time to find out how good they are. If their probation period ends before you have made a decision, you're not allowed to fire them; you need to give them more training instead. Do you see the resemblance with parenting here?

5. **Don't let your emotions get involved.** It's often best to engage someone to support you through the recruitment process, such as your accountant. He or she can check the employee handbook and make sure the protocol is being followed.

6. **Use disciplinary procedures.** Sometimes, following disciplinary procedures is more suitable than dismissing an employee. This process takes time: depending on your policy, you will first have an appraisal meeting where you will highlight the problem to the employee. This is usually followed by a period of training, after which you will need to evaluate the employee's work. If the employee has made improvements and you're satisfied that they are able to do the job, you won't need to take

further action. If they are still unable to fulfil their role, as long as you have followed the disciplinary procedure, you will be within your rights to dismiss them.

7. **Make sure you're clear about employment law and how it works.** You can avoid a lot of stress and wasted time if you deal with issues at an early stage and use the legal processes available to you. You, as an employer, should be as equipped as possible, because in the worst-case scenario a disgruntled employee will have easy access to legal aid. There are plenty of sources of guidance, protection and help for employees who want to build a case against you. Many companies offer these services for free because they earn their commission when they win a case, so you can imagine how incentivised they are. Curious? Visit https:// employmenttribunal.claims/about-us or type 'Got the boot' into Google.

Acccountants

That's right: acccountants. It's not a mistake. I'm talking about people who pretend to be accountants, and the need to protect your business from them. Accountancy is a regulated profession, and accountants need to have qualifications, have professional indemnity insurance and be registered with HMRC if they are to liaise with HMRC on your behalf. Not everyone who does accounts is a qualified accountant. If you're going to sign the accounts as the director of your business, you have to be sure of your accountant's credentials.

CASE STUDY: WORKING WITH THE WRONG PEOPLE

Recently, a local factory asked my company to finalise their accounts. Their accounts were due to be filed, but their previous accountant had disappeared and the team at the factory were unable to get hold of him.

The client's books were run in Sage (bookkeeping software) and they looked normal and legitimate. My team prepared and finalised their financial statements and then filed them, and the client was happy. A few months later, though, they began receiving letters from HMRC stating that they owed a lot of money.

The client asked me to get involved. It took me and my team... wait for it... eighteen months to get to the root of the issue. HMRC requested bank statements, receipts, payments and payslips, and information about transactions. They even visited the client. It was only when HMRC asked for a breakdown of where payments had been made that we realised what had happened to the money: fraudsters had gained access to the company's bank accounts via the accountant, who had diverted the funds. More than £200,000 had been diverted to the fraudsters' bank accounts and the accountant made it look like the payments had been sent to HMRC instead.

It's important to make sure you don't out-source the financial part of your business to an accountant with a triple 'c'. You can do this by asking them what professional body they are registered with. They should present you with an HMRC form 64-8 which, once duly completed and signed by you, will give them authority to represent you in any dealings with HMRC. Ask to see their professional indemnity insurance too, so you know that they have the appropriate protection in place.

HMRC

You may be surprised to learn that you have to protect your business from HMRC. Based on the HMRC Annual Report and Accounts for 2017–2018 and 2018–2019 the number of full-time equivalent employees recruited in 2017–18 was 4,604 and in 2018–19 it was 5,830.[23] That's an increase of 26%. Considering that there is a strong trend on automating and digitalising, we can conclude that more and more people are working for the tax office, and they are not in their call centres. HMRC can open a tax review of your business within six years of the end of the accounting period or the date you filed the tax return, whichever is later. This rule applies to personal affairs and limited companies, so you need to keep

2   www.gov.uk/government/publications/hmrc-annual-report-and-accounts-2017-to-2018

3   www.gov.uk/government/publications/hmrc-annual-report-and-accounts-2018-to-2019

records for both of these for six years. There are harsh tax consequences and strict penalties if you don't provide the information you're asked for.

The best way to protect your business is to keep your books and records in order, but even when they're in pristine condition, having a tax officer scrutinise them can be a stressful experience. The best way to handle this is to remove yourself from the direct line of fire. If you've ever played chess, it's the equivalent to hiding the king behind another piece. Put your accountant on the front line to deal with the HMRC inspectors so that you can get on with running your business.

You'll need to pay for the accountant's time and expertise in dealing with the HMRC investigation, but fee protection insurance will cover that cost. You will be compensated for the time that your accountant has to spend on the case, which is usually at least fifteen hours. The policy won't cover tax liabilities and penalties, because if something has been done wrong then the company will have to pay for it. If it was your accountant who made a mistake, you might have grounds to ask the accountant to pay for that and then they would handle it with their professional indemnity insurance.

This is why you need to do your due diligence before outsourcing your accounts to anyone.

Fraudsters

You need to make sure that you're protected in case you are the victim of fraud. A common type of fraud is when you receive an email, text or phone call from someone pretending to be an HMRC inspector. The fraudster asks you to disclose personal details so that they can investigate a fraudulent transaction, or they might demand payment of tax which is a long time overdue. They will try to manipulate you in the conversation to make such payments. It will sound very realistic. Although this type of fraud has been significantly reduced, there are still many cases of it happening. If you receive a request like this, take the name of the person who calls you, make sure you don't give them any personal details and contact your accountant immediately. They will then tell you if the request is genuine or fraudulent. Fraudulent texts and emails look exactly the same as HMRC's, but if you hover your cursor over the email address it was sent from, it will not show genuine HMRC details.

Now that all the pieces of the protection jigsaw are in place, you need the glue that will hold them together: get your vision and strategy out of your head and put it down on paper for others to see. This means creating a manual, systems and processes that will enable your business to function, with or without you in it. When your business becomes self-functioning, you can concentrate more and more on strategy, rather than getting your feet caught in the weeds of day-to-day business operations. You will be surprised by how much further you can take your business once you're able to step back. When you're so close to your business, it can be difficult to see what's wrong with it; as soon as you extract yourself, you can take your business to the next level of possibility.

Summary

The right accountant is more important to your business than you might think. A good accountant can do more than just put figures together: they can advise you on the performance of the business and, more importantly, they can protect you in difficult situations with employees, HMRC and fraud. Acting as an intermediary here is the extra value that your accountant can bring.

EXERCISE: ARE WE PROTECTED?

Now that you have finished reading this chapter, take a few moments to complete this exercise. Think carefully about the following questions and try to answer clearly.

Which three areas in your business do you feel are most vulnerable?

For each, think about your strategy for dealing with it. How can you tackle this vulnerability? Who needs to be involved? What are the specific actions you need to take?

Summary

I hope you have enjoyed *Rewire Your Business For Success* and, most importantly, that you have implemented the strategy and refined your view of your business. These principles will change your business and your life forever. There is a temptation to follow them all at once, and if you feel strong and you have a team to support you then go for it! There is no one-size-fits-all. Some of my clients like to complete one principle and wait until it is fully embedded before moving on to the next one. Others like to blitz through and see an avalanche of results: if their head isn't spinning, they aren't going fast enough.

However you prefer to implement the model, I urge you to keep going with the changes to take your business to the next level.

Given the input into so many businesses and the great feedback I have received, I believe this model will help any business that wants to progress. If you've implemented these six principles correctly, you will have stopped chasing money and you will know that the model will help you increase your profit and give you the freedom to live the life you choose. We all develop bad habits over the years, and those repeated patterns will have been keeping your business stuck in a rut. When you apply the six principles, you will change your patterns of behaviour and move towards your desired outcomes.

I know this method works because I have applied it to my own business, but it is not an easy ride. In fact, it is hard work to break old patterns and introduce new changes. Reading this book is just the start of your journey: to get real control over your business, you need to take action and implement your strategy every step of the way. Don't worry about getting things wrong or you will become trapped in paralysis analysis. A well-executed plan today is much better than the perfect plan that is never executed. Once you take that action, you'll be amazed by how the model transforms your business. My clients have even told me that their personal relationships have improved after following the six principles, as they're less stressed and have more time to focus on what's really important.

CASE STUDY: A TRANSFORMATION

One client was elated by the recent work that I did with him to implement the model. It took three months to work through the six principles. He was a dedicated and hard-working business owner, but he was continuously chasing his tail. The excitement about starting his business had begun to fade; on some days he was fatigued and had no desire to go to the office; and he had no savings, no holidays and no joy in life.

When I suggested that he apply the six principles he was resistant to change, but eventually he agreed to follow the whole process. I recently received a phone call from him to tell me that he was delighted! He had just checked his account and found that he had £24,000 in accumulated funds. This was not money that he needed to live on; it was a fund set aside for him to invest.

In five years of running a business, he had never managed to accumulate so much; what's more, he no longer had any debt. On top of that, he called us from another country where he was on holiday – something he hadn't been able to do for a long time. He felt more confident about his business, his team were happier and he was excited about the future.

What to do next

Implement the six principles to rewire your business for success, taking each step one at a time. If you encounter any problems, please feel free to reach out by email so I can help you resolve them.

Don't forget to complete your scorecard at www.rewire4success.com/book/scorecard and get your report. This will be your starting point for establishing where your business is at this moment in time.

Contact me

Follow me on Instagram at ElenaMeskhiAndCo, where I share many tips and insights about business and the business owner's life.

Email me on contact@rewire4success.com to let me know how you are getting on, or if you get stuck or want to be inspired.

Visit my book website at www.rewire4success. com to find out more about the work I do for my clients and get the bonus material mentioned in this book.

Finally, spread the word. I know this model works, and I want to share it with as many business owners as possible so that they, too, can create the business and the life that they truly want.

Acknowledgements

To acknowledge everyone who influenced or contributed to this book is a difficult task.

I thank the many people who made it real for me. Daniel and Andrew Priestley and Glen Carlson for pushing me out of my comfort zone; Lucy McCarraher and the team at Rethink Press for their experience and advice.

This book is for my team. Thanks to each and every member who got stuff done while

I was concentrating on my writing – Rinata, Hannah, Alena, Kirsty, Saffi, Batool, Faith, Krystyna, Kate the list goes on.

Thanks to my clients for their loyalty and their continuous supply of case studies and experience.

Thanks to my family, for their granite support and their faith that I would get this done.

To my kids, for fun when I needed the distraction. For their childlike determination to get that Lego spider assembled and the numerous analogies I picked up from them. The mantra my kids love: I can do it, I will do it, and I never give up.

This book was able to see the light of day thanks to all of you. My big, sincere, heartfelt thanks!

The Author

Elena Meskhi is a certified accountant and tax advisor who leads a team of accountants and tax advisors in the firm Elena Meskhi & Co. Elena is also a non-executive director on the board of several companies, where she contributes her expertise and experience in running a business.

Seven out of ten businesses close down within five years, mainly because of leader burnout, running out of cash or a lack of support from the team.[4, 5] When this happens, other areas of the business owner's life suffer – their family, their children and their community. It's difficult for the business owner to overcome their feelings of failure. But it doesn't have to be that way. Taking a business forward is a strategic, predictable stage of its development. Drawing on examples from her clients' and her own businesses, Elena uses science, experience and economics to bring business development strategy to the next level. In this book she reveals her formula for taking your business to the next stage of development without burnout, stress or negativity. Don't leave the success of your business to chance. Get in the driving seat and go for it!

Ⓜ contact@rewire4success.com

Ⓘ ElenaMeskhiAndCo

⊕ www.rewire4success.com

---

4   www.telegraph.co.uk/politics/2019/01/24/start-ups-across-uk-going-bust-need-careful-management-economy
5   www.forbes.com/sites/forbesfinancecouncil/2018/10/25/what-percentage-of-small-businesses-fail-and-how-can-you-avoid-being-one-of-them/#11226dca43b5